PHILOSOPHICAL HERMENEUTICS AND LITERARY THEORY

PHILOSOPHICAL

HERMENEUTICS

AND LITERARY

THEORY

JOEL WEINSHEIMER

YALE UNIVERSITY PRESS

NEW HAVEN & LONDON

Designed by Richard Hendel.
Set in Sabon type by
Keystone Typesetting, Inc., Orwigsburg, Pennsylvania.
Printed in the United States of America by
BookCrafters, Chelsea, Michigan.

Library of Congress Cataloging-in-Publication Data
Weinsheimer, Joel.
    Philosophical hermeneutics and literary theory / Joel Weinsheimer.
        p.   cm.
    Includes bibliographical references and index.
    ISBN 0-300-04785-1
        1. Hermeneutics. 2. Gadamer, Hans Georg, 1900–   —
Contributions in hermeneutics. 3. Literature—Philosophy. I. Title.
    BD241.W44   1991
    121'.68'092—dc20
                                                            90-39159
                                                            CIP

The paper in this book meets the guidelines for permanence and
durability of the Committee on Production Guidelines for Book
Longevity of the Council on Library Resources.

10 9 8 7 6 5 4 3 2 1

For Hans-Georg Gadamer

CONTENTS

PREFACE

"Philosophical hermeneutics," in the narrow sense, refers specifically to Hans-Georg Gadamer's account of understanding, since he has applied the term to his own work—notably in the subtitle of *Wahrheit und Methode: Grundzüge einer philoso-phischen Hermeneutik.* Though "philosophical hermeneutics" might well be extended to include the ideas of Heidegger, Ricoeur, and various others as well, here I will focus on Gadamer in particular. My hope in this, as in my previous work on Gadamer, is to broaden his influence by demonstrating the fruitfulness of his thought. This book is not critical in intent; its purpose is not to review or appraise Gadamer's hermeneutics generally. That has already been done particularly well by a number of others, most recently Georgia Warnke. The field of philosophical hermeneutics has perhaps been sufficiently mapped and tilled; now is harvest time. By this I do not mean it is time to apply Gadamer's principles in order to make the practice of interpretation more efficient, accurate, or philosophically defensible. Rather, at this juncture we are pre-pared to discern how his insights alter our understanding of under-standing as it occurs in particular areas of hermeneutic endeavor. Susan Noakes has observed that "despite the cross-disciplinary breadth of Gadamer's influence, attempts to integrate his ideas into literary criticism have been few" (*Timely Reading,* 231). Gerald Bruns's *Inventions* must be numbered prominently among these few.

And the present book is also such an attempt. Its aim is to explore and extend the contributions of philosophical hermeneutics to literary theory and interpretation, broadly conceived.

The survey of modern hermeneutics with which I begin in chapter 1 makes it apparent that Gadamer's work represents neither the first nor the last word in hermeneutics but is instead situated in the middle of an ongoing dialogue. This lack of finality is not unique or accidental; it characterizes post-romantic hermeneutics generally. Stipulating no interpretive canon, no fixed system of rules, principles, or guidelines, modern hermeneutics is not finally to be distinguished from the continuing history of what it has been interpreted to be. Like all things historical, hermeneutics cannot be understood apart from our changing conceptions of what it is. To survey the history of the various and in part conflicting understandings from Schleiermacher to Ricoeur is not, then, to overlook modern hermeneutics in itself but rather precisely to see it.

Hermeneutics acquired a new conception of itself when, in Kantian fashion, Schleiermacher shifted its task from establishing practical guidelines for understanding to discovering the general conditions that make it possible to understand at all. Gadamer has completed this shift by making his hermeneutics specifically philosophical, distinguishing it from hermeneutic theory in the strict sense and therefore also from literary theory insofar as hermeneutic theory is part of it. If, as has recently been suggested, literary theory consists in the attempt to regulate interpretation by appeal to a general conception of literature and the interpretation of it, then Gadamer's hermeneutics is not theoretical. It is in fact anti-theoretical in one respect, for it explores how understanding occurs at all— not how it should be regulated in order to function more rigorously or effectively. Indeed, one of Gadamer's fundamental insights occurs in explaining why theory of interpretation is of itself limited in scope. Ultimately, he shows, understanding is not governed by method: it is not fully susceptible of control, being something that happens to the interpreter. As I show in chapter 2, for Gadamer understanding (philosophically considered) is an effect of history, not finally an action but a passion.

If history is thus the condition of understanding, it is also its subject matter; and to explain the nature of history in this latter sense Gadamer draws on Kant's third critique to develop what I call an aesthetics of history, which is examined in chapter 3. He is not, of course, concerned with a feeling of pleasure in the events of history or what is written about them. Rather, in part I of *Truth and Method* Gadamer is suggesting that the kind of judgment Kant reserved for the aesthetic is also required in understanding history. Against neo-classical aesthetics, Kant contended that beauty cannot be decided by rules but only by the reflective judgment that he elaborates in the *Critique of Judgment*. Such judgment consists not in merely applying a preexistent and fixed rule to decide whether something is beautiful; on the contrary, the rule is determined and defined in the very process of applying it. Like the beautiful, Gadamer contends, the historical cannot be understood as the mere instantiation of a general rule or law, for history is essentially particular. Thus understanding history, too, requires reflective judgment. Gadamer's aesthetics of history implies that to understand the historical particular as something other than a case subsumed under a law is to understand it as in part productive of the law that applies to it.

What we need, then, is a new conception of historical understanding, one that avoids the pitfalls of the old model, which emphasized subsuming particulars under generals. Gadamer's model, the fusion of horizons, at first appears to offer no solution, since the notion of fusion (like that of subsumption) seems to ignore or repress particularity. Its whole point is apparently to supersede difference. But what Gadamer means by fusion, I think, is something like the nonrepressive relation of tenor and vehicle that occurs in metaphor. Gadamer speaks of the metaphoricity of language in general; and if, as he contends, language makes understanding possible, its metaphoricity must be reflected in understanding itself. In chapter 4 I show that what Richards and Black, as well as Ricoeur and Derrida, have discovered concerning the nature of metaphor can be appropriated hermeneutically to describe the nature of interpretive understanding. Conceived metaphorically, interpretation is a union of the same and the different. Like metaphor, understanding ideally maintains both the identity and the nonidentity of the vehicle and tenor, the interpreter's horizon and that of the text to be understood.

The relation of the interpreter's language to the text is not unique or special; it is fundamentally the same relation as that which always obtains between words and things. For this reason, it is not enough to emphasize their difference, as Saussurean semiology has done. Gadamer finds that the similarity theory of language, rejected at least since Plato's *Cratylus*, still has some truth to it. A word, he concludes, is something like an image—that is, it belongs to what it represents, as a mirror image belongs to what it mirrors. A word, therefore, is not just a sign, as chapter 5 explains.

Finally, I examine how the union of sameness and difference that is manifest in interpretive language and all language bears on the current debate concerning the canon. I do not pretend that philosophical hermeneutics can resolve this dispute. Quite the opposite, its effect may well be to prolong it, for the value of philosophical hermeneutics in the context of the classic lies not so much in providing answers as in opening up questions that have not been fully considered. In chapter 6 I outline three such questions: in regard to the classic, how do we maintain the dialogue between the work and its reader without silencing either? how can we combine historical continuity and discontinuity without denying either? and, considering what it means to call the classic a sacred text, how do we think truth and power together without reducing one to the other?

What is the common thread in the contributions of philosophical hermeneutics to literary theory? Wordsworth states it quite precisely. Among the chief causes of the pleasure we take in poetry, he remarks in the 1850 preface to *Lyrical Ballads*, "is to be reckoned a principle which must be well known to those who have made any of the arts the object of accurate reflection: namely, the pleasure which the mind derives from the perception of similitude in dissimilitude. This principle is the great spring of the activity of our minds" (1:149). Wordsworth here sounds the dominant note to which hermeneutic reflection always recurs: the multifaceted tension between the one and the many. In metaphor and application, in the complex dialogue between the past and present, and between the interpretation and the interpreted generally—in all of these is to be discerned the irreducible interplay of sameness and difference. If our time tends to celebrate plurality, diversity, and even conflict, the contrary impulse toward unity and unanimity cannot be long in reasserting itself. What philosophical hermeneutics reminds us, however, is that both extremes, homogeneity and heterogeneity alike, deaden mental activity. For understanding lives in the play of equivalence and difference.

To a number of friends and colleagues I owe a debt of gratitude for their contributions to this project. Chapters 2, 3, and 4 were written for presentation at various colloquia at the kind invitations of Joseph Buttigieg, Wlad Godzich, and Donald Marshall respectively. With the generous support of a University of Minnesota Graduate School grant, Chip Burkitt and Michael Gareffa assisted untiringly in preparing the manuscript. I cannot let pass this opportunity to express my thanks to Ellen Graham, whose graciousness, sound judgment, and good sense have not only been invaluable to me personally but have set the standard of professionalism in scholarly publishing for many years. An earlier version of chapter 1 appeared in G. Douglas Atkins and Laurie Morrow, eds., *Contemporary Critical Theory* (Amherst: University of Massachusetts Press, 1989), 117–36. Chapter 4 appears in Hugh J. Silverman, ed., *Gadamer and Hermeneutics* (London: Routledge and Kegan Paul, 1991) and in the *Journal of Literary Studies*.

PHILOSOPHICAL
HERMENEUTICS
AND LITERARY
THEORY

I

MODERN HERMENEUTICS:

AN INTRODUCTORY

OVERVIEW

Hermeneutics is the theory and practice of interpretation. Its province extends as far as does meaning and the need to understand it. Hermeneutics names no particular method of interpretation or coherent body of theory that could be expounded in systematic form. In our time, as before, it exists only as a historical tradition. Thus hermeneutics can be understood only through a historical overview of its development.

In the form of philology, exegesis, and commentary, hermeneutics had its origin in the allegorical interpretation of Homer, beginning in the sixth century B.C., and in rabbinic midrash and commentary on the Torah. Influenced by both the Homeric and the Jewish tradition, Christian hermeneutics is commonly dated from Philo Judaeus, who, in the first century, methodized interpretation of the Bible in a way that influenced not only Origen, Augustine, and many others before the Reformation but also Dilthey and Betti long afterward. The four-tiered hierarchy of meanings appeared as early as the fifth century, and the typological, moral, and anagogical interpretations that it introduced are still employed in churches today. Hermeneutics began, then, with the interpretation of canonical texts—including the Homeric epics—and even in our time it has not entirely lost sight of the aim that motivates all scriptural interpretation: to disclose not just fact but truth. Yet now the domain of hermeneutics is perceived to reach well beyond theology and philology—into sociology, aesthetics, historiography, law, and the human sciences generally. And considering that post-positivist philosophy has begun to acknowledge the role of hermeneutic understanding in the natural sciences as well, there is good reason to take seriously Gadamer's claim that the scope of hermeneutics is universal.

This broadening of hermeneutics, from a local and ancillary exegetical aid to a mode of understanding so fundamental as to be universal, involves more than quantitative extension. A fairly clear, though not abrupt, qualitative shift occurred in the late eighteenth century, when the coincidence of classical and biblical modes of interpretation could no longer be taken for granted. "Hermeneutics as the art of understanding does not yet exist in general," Friedrich Schleiermacher wrote in the outline of his 1819 lectures; "rather, only various specialized hermeneutics exist" (1). Thus the need had become evident for a comprehensive theory, uniting not only classical and biblical but indeed all interpretive activities, regardless of their subject matter. Because he was the first to focus on the general principles of understanding, as something more than an aid for specific difficulties, Schleiermacher is credited with being the progenitor of modern hermeneutics.

The significance of Schleiermacher's program does not lie solely in its description of specific cross-disciplinary methods, although his methods were unusually influential. More important, perhaps, is the fact that his hermeneutics, intended to cover every sphere of interpretation, was constructed apart from any particular sphere. What occasioned Schleiermacher's efforts were not the obstacles specific to understanding some particular canon but rather the fact that understanding itself had become problematical and in need of assistance. We cannot assume that the effort of interpretation results naturally in understanding, Schleiermacher contends. Quite the contrary, "strict interpretation begins with misunderstanding" (8). For this reason, his hermeneutics devotes itself to the means of avoiding misunderstanding. Schleiermacher attempts not so much to understand understanding as to guide it, to methodize it, and to produce artificially the understanding that does not occur naturally.

Correct interpretation, in Schleiermacher's view, requires a regulated re-creation of the creation to be understood. Since no creation is consciously constructed by rule (for example, we follow but do not think about the rules of syntax in speaking), the re-creator who does reconstruct a text on the basis of its implicit rules can understand it better than its author did. But though rule-governed, the task of reconstruction, as Schleiermacher envisions it, is by no means mechanical or certain of its results. It involves two types of reconstruction. The first is variously called grammatical, historical, or comparative reconstruction. For Schleiermacher, the paradigmatic object of interpretation is a text. And just as a word in the text can be understood only in relation to its context in the sentence, so also the part-whole version of the hermeneutic circle applies to wider contexts: the relation of the text to the author's canon, of the canon to the language, and of the language to other languages and to previous and subsequent history generally. "Posed in this manner, the task is an infinite one, because there is an infinity of the past and the future that we wish to see in the moment of discourse" (10). Since "no inspection of a work ever exhausts its meaning" (14), it follows that every interpretation is finite and therefore provisional; but the interpretation is finite because the meaning of every work is infinite.

Second, in Schleiermacher's view the re-creation of the author's creation requires divinatory reconstruction, which is not merely supplemental to but inseparable from contextual reconstruction. "Using the divinatory [method], one seeks to understand the writer immediately to the point that one transforms oneself into the other" (14). Even if the meaning of a work is infinite because infinitely contextualizable, the meaning is determinate because it is the creation of a particular author on a particular occasion. The interpreter of a given text cannot be content with understanding what contemporaneous authors typically thought, or even with what this author characteristically wrote; rather, the objective of interpretation is to determine what this author means in this specific text. The understanding of an original and creative author cannot be mediated solely by the typical and characteristic; it also necessitates immediate understanding of the particular as particular, and this intuitive or empathic understanding Schleiermacher calls divination. To understand the other as such, interpreters take their inspiration from the universal traits of human nature that they too possess, but further they must make a sympathetic leap beyond themselves and even beyond the common and shared. In this way individual interpreters become the individual creators whom they interpret.

Schleiermacher's concern to lay down the guidelines of correct interpretation was preserved and intensified by his biographer and intellectual heir, Wilhelm Dilthey. But Dilthey conceived the task of providing a methodology, a general theory of valid understanding, as prior to that of specifying the methods or rules of intepretation. Complicating Dilthey's methodological task and giving rise to it were two factors: first, an acute sense of the achievements of the Historical School, including not only Ranke and Droysen but even Hegel, and, second, Dilthey's no less acute sense of the achievements of natural science and the success of Kant's attempts to legitimate it. Both factors are at work in Dilthey's contention that hermeneutics

has, beyond its use in the business of interpretation, a second task which is indeed its main one: it is to counteract the constant irruption of romantic whim and sceptical subjectivity into the realm of history by laying the historical foundations of valid interpretation on which all certainty in history rests. Absorbed into the context of the epistemology, logic and methodology of the human studies, the theory of interpretation becomes a vital link between philosophy and the historical disciplines, an essential part of the foundations of the studies of man. [*Selected Writings*, 260]

The several "studies of man" that Dilthey attempted to ground by means of his methodology originated during the Enlightenment when "the general system of history was divided up into individual systems—like those of law, religion, or poetry." (205). Insofar as "history" means legal, religious, literary, or other history, it is only one among many human sciences. Yet after Winckelmann, philosophical and empirical historians began "treating history as the source of all mind-constructed facts" (159). Historical development, in this view, belongs intrinsically to all the human sciences, for it is only historically that the human can be understood. Schleiermacher's philological hermeneutics, though limited to no particular kind of text, was yet text-oriented. Dilthey affirms and expands Schleiermacher's insight—that essentially intelligible entities are texts—to include all historical phenomena. Every product of objective mind, every product of culture, including nonverbal records, must and can be understood as a text. As one expression of objective mind, historiography too has its source in history. If there is to be validity in interpreting the great book of history—if one is to resist "romantic whim and sceptical subjectivity"—the very certainty of historical interpretation itself must rest on historical foundations. History is self-certifying; that is, history is a ground of truth.

It seems that for Dilthey, nevertheless, history was not a sufficient ground, because he also suggests that hermeneutics needs to be "absorbed into the context of the epistemology, logic and methodology of the human studies" (260). This absorption necessitates a rational rather than historical grounding; it was to have been accomplished in Dilthey's *Critique of Historical Reason*, but the critique was never completed. This work was intended to show the conditions and limits of historical knowledge, just as Kant's first critique had demonstrated those of natural science. Among Dilthey's

main ambitions was to distinguish the foundations of the human
sciences from those of the natural and yet to make them no less solid.
Thus, like other neo-Kantians, Dilthey distinguished understanding
from explanation, and he based the human sciences on understanding, while attempting to justify understanding epistemologically.

For Kant the main problem in demonstrating the intelligibility of
nature occurred in applying the unifying categories to the manifold
of experience, which he solved through his transcendental schemata.
Because of the absence of lawlike causality in the historical world,
however, Dilthey found that Kant's transcendental solution could
not be transposed to explain the validity of historical knowledge.
And in fact it did not need to be transferred, because historical
knowledge possesses a more immediate ground of intelligibility and
reliability than natural science. This ground Dilthey discerned in the
unity of historical life itself:

> Life consists of parts, of experiences which are inwardly related
> to each other. Every particular experience refers to a self of
> which it is a part; it is structurally interrelated to other parts.
> Everything which pertains to mind is interrelated: interconnect-
> edness is, therefore, a category originating from life. We ap-
> prehend connectedness through the unity of consciousness
> which is the condition of all apprehension. However, connect-
> edness clearly does not follow from the fact of a manifold of
> experiences being presented to a unitary consciousness. Only
> because life is itself a structural connection of experiences—i.e.,
> experienced relations—is the connectedness of life given. [211]

The historical world exhibits intrinsic connection and relation
among experiences instead of displaying the external, causal relation among events that characterizes the natural world. Like all
organic life, experiences cannot be decomposed into more elemen-
tary units, such as discrete sensations, whose synthesis would then
require explanation; rather, historical experience is already coherent. The understanding of it necessitates no imposition of alien

unities because experiences are in themselves structurally connected to other experiences, and are therefore intrinsically intelligible. The hermeneutic relation of part and whole inheres not only in the interpretive apprehension of the knowing subject but also in the object known: historical life itself is an organic, intrinsically understandable text.

Whereas Schleiermacher contributed substantially to the general methods of the science of interpretation, and Dilthey to the methodology of the human sciences broadly conceived, Heidegger did not primarily intend to contribute anything further to either level of science. Yet he builds on his predecessors' efforts. "Scientific research," Heidegger writes, "is not the only manner of Being which [*Dasein*] can have, nor is it the one which lies closest" [*Being and Time*, 32). "Dilthey's own researches for laying the basis for the human sciences were forced one-sidedly into the field of theory of science" (450), Heidegger acknowledges. His own analysis of the problem of history nevertheless arises "in the process of appropriating the labors of Dilthey" (449) because "the 'logic of the human sciences' was by no means central to [Dilthey]" (450). Rather than this logic, what Heidegger learns from Dilthey is that hermeneutics names not just the methodology of the human sciences but something more fundamental to Dasein than any science. Heidegger's project is not epistemological but ontological, and for him understanding is not only a way of knowing but also of being. Thus he extends the object of hermeneutic understanding beyond individual texts and all other historical entities to an understanding of being.

In *Being and Time* hermeneutics figures as both the mode of inquiry and the subject matter; and these are necessarily, even circularly, interrelated. The cardinal aim of *Being and Time* is to reopen the "question of the meaning of Being in general" (61). Simply put, What does it mean to be? Because the answer to this question is a meaning, it is to be discovered in the way all meaning is discovered: by interpretation. Heidegger's ontology does not consist merely in describing phenomena (modes of givenness); additionally, it is concerned with what has been covered up (preeminently the question of the meaning of being). "Covered-up-ness," Heidegger writes, "is the counter-concept to 'phenomenon'" (60). To disclose what is covered up, description does not suffice. Heidegger's phenomenology is therefore hermeneutic: first because its aim is meaning, and second because this meaning needs to be un-covered. That un-covering is the function of interpretation.

Interpretation operates in the liminal space between the hidden and the open, the concealed and the revealed. Since it cannot begin ex nihilo, it needs a clue; and if hermeneutic ontology is to uncover the meaning of being, then that meaning "must already be available to us in some way" (25). If it were not somehow already available, all ontological interpretation would be impossible and the whole project of *Being and Time* would be futile. If the meaning of being is even vaguely familiar, however, that fact is in itself highly significant, for it implies that "understanding of Being is a definite characteristic of Dasein's being" (32). Dasein is distinct from all other beings in that its own being is an issue for it, which indicates that it has at least a dim intimation of what it means to be. Thus *Being and Time* takes the being of Dasein as the clue to the meaning of being.

To take a being as the clue to being is manifestly not a presuppositionless mode of inquiry; quite the opposite, it is circular. Circular reasoning is open to obvious objections; at the same time, it finds its own kind of rigor in "working out [its] fore-structures in terms of the things themselves" (195), and this is what Heidegger has done. His own inquiry into the being of Dasein is circular, no doubt, but so is Dasein itself: "An entity for which . . . its being is itself an issue, has, ontologically, a circular structure" (195). There is thus an exact coincidence between Heidegger's method and its object:

> Like any ontological Interpretation whatsoever, this analytic can only, so to speak, "listen in" to some previously disclosed entity as regards its Being. And it will attach itself to Dasein's distinctive and most far-reaching possibilities of disclosure, in

order to get information about this entity from these. Phenomenological Interpretation must make it possible for Dasein itself
to disclose things primordially; it must, as it were, let Dasein
interpret itself. [179]

Dasein—this circular being distinguished by its understanding of
being—interprets itself. Such interpretation is not introspective self-
interpretation; nor is Heidegger here thinking of human being as an
object of the human or natural sciences. Instead he is concerned with
elucidating a more primordial kind of interpretation from which all
interpretation and science derive. As a mode of Dasein's being, understanding designates a way of being in the world that is collo-
quially called know-how, knowing the ropes, or being in the know.
So conceived, understanding consists not in knowing this or that but
in being familiar with an entirety of relations in such a way that
within them one can do, make, and know, even without reflection.
Against this background of pre-reflective practices in which there is
neither subject nor object, all reflective cognition and interpretation
takes place.

Dasein, as understanding, "knows" what everything in its world
can be used for, its significance and possibility; and the same is true
of Dasein itself as a being in the world. "Understanding 'knows'
what it is capable of—that is, what its potentiality-for-Being is
capable of" (184). Potentiality, possibility, capability belongs to
what Dasein not only can be, but already is. The being of Dasein as
understanding consists in being able—not just in being able to do
such and such but in being able to be. In a sense, Dasein never is, but
always is to be. In every present, its being is futural, as it projects in
understanding what other things and itself can be. Yet its present is
also past, since understanding needs a clue. In other words, Dasein
projects its being on the basis of the background practices that are
called historical context or tradition. Dasein already (past) understands what it is (present) to be (future).

The coming to be—the unfolding or explication—of what Dasein

can be Heidegger calls interpretation. "In interpretation, understanding does not become something different. It becomes itself.
Such interpretation is grounded existentially in understanding; the
latter does not arise from the former. Nor is interpretation the
acquiring of information about what is to be understood; it is rather
the working-out of possibilities projected in understanding" (188–
89). We need to remember that Heidegger is not here describing
literary, historical, or other kinds of reflexive interpretation, yet
what he says has an obvious bearing on them. "Any interpretation
which is to contribute understanding, must already have understood
what is to be interpreted. This is a fact that has always been remarked, even if only in the area of derivative ways of understanding
and interpretation, such as philological Interpretation" (194). Traditionally the hermeneutic circle has been expressed in spatial terms
of part and whole. Heidegger, by contrast, thinks of it temporally, in
terms of a circle between the "already" and the "to be." This cir-
cularity, moreover, is not a merit or defect peculiar to the interpretive sciences but rather corresponds to the historical being of Dasein
from which these sciences and all other modes of understanding
derive. The whole that is projected before the parts are understood is
a whole historical world, a familiar network of significances, a past
world already understood that is continually modified in interpretation. Simply put, life is interpretation. The coming to be of what
Dasein can be is its self-interpretation, and this interpretive proliferation of being progresses toward no fullness or finality. It simply
continues until Dasein itself ceases.

When Rudolf Bultmann took up Heidegger's analysis of understanding in order to explain the nature of biblical interpretation, the
result was a theory that stressed the existential appropriation of the
meaning of scripture. To understand the kerygma is to discover a
possibility for changing one's life, for altering what one is. Understanding the Word of God means understanding it as a call to
salvation, that is, as an invitation to authentic existence; and under-

standing a call in this way involves not just knowing what the Word means but heeding it, whether by acceptance or rejection. The New Testament is itself one existential appropriation of the kerygma, specifically that of the early Christians; but it is neither the only nor the definitive one. Rather than the Word of God itself, scripture is an initial interpretation of the Word, one expressed in a mythic language appropriate to its initial audience. Because mythic explications of the saving Word are now largely incredible, understanding the kerygma today requires a demythologization. Far from debunking the kerygma or exposing its pretenses, demythologization allows the call to be heard and heeded.

Like the early Christians, however, we can interpret and appropriate the Word of God because we pre-understand it; we already know what it would mean to be saved, already recognize the poverty of our existence and believe in the possibility of enriching it. This belief, common to all people though more intense in some, is the precondition of interpretive understanding. Suppressing pre-understanding therefore does not promote correct interpretation but simply renders the text nonsensical and unintelligible. Denying the prior claim of the Word cannot be the condition of rightly understanding it. The interpreter's pre-understanding needs rather to be brought into play, tested, and examined. Interpreters need to allow their very being to be called into question in the same process by which they question the text. For Bultmann it is not finally paradoxical to say that the most subjective interpretation, the one that hits closest to home, is always the most objective.

Precisely this integration of subjectivity and objectivity caused Emilio Betti to charge that Bultmann espouses what is ultimately a subjectivist hermeneutics: it lacks any means for certifying the correctness of interpretation, and in fact encourages the worst kind of sheer projection. Much in the line of Schleiermacher and Dilthey, Betti writes that "it is our duty as guardians and practitioners of the study of history to protect . . . objectivity and to provide evidence of the epistemological conditions of its possibility" ("Hermeneutics," 73). Betti acknowledges the principle of the "actuality of under-standing," namely that in order to understand a past event one must assimilate it "into one's intellectual horizon within the framework of one's own experiences" (62). But Bultmann's mistake, Betti argues, is to neglect another, no less fundamental principle: the autonomy of the object. The object of interpretation is the objectification of a mind not our own; the aim of interpretation is to understand what someone else did or thought or wrote, not what we did. The object of interpretation must therefore be understood immanently, accord-ing to its own logic, not ours. The danger of Bultmann's approach lies in the potential for "deriving only what is meaningful or reason-able to oneself and of missing what is different and specific in the Other or, as the case may be, bracketing it as a presumed myth" (73). For Betti, by contrast, the other's alienness to the interpreter occa-sions interpretation in the first place; and just as this alterity necessi-tates objectivity in interpretation, so it makes objectivity possible. The possibility of objective interpretation should be preserved by sharply separating two questions that Bultmann confused: the "question concerning the meaning of an historical phenomenon" and the "completely different question . . . concerning its present *Bedeutsamkeit* (significance) and relevance in changing historical epochs" (68).[1] Both kinds of inquiry are necessary. Perhaps the question of significance is even more important; but answering it, in Betti's view, first requires objectively determining the meaning in itself.

Betti similarly criticizes Hans-Georg Gadamer, who (like Bult-mann) builds on the insights of Heidegger, and not just the early Heidegger of *Being and Time* but also the later Heidegger, after his turn to language. In *Truth and Method* Gadamer too seeks to dis-

---

1. This Fregean distinction plays an important role in the work of E. D. Hirsch as well.

close the grounds of the possibility of true interpretation; but from his point of view Betti's position rather than Bultmann's appears subjectivist—not despite Betti's objectivism, but because of it. From Gadamer's perspective, objectivism and subjectivism amount to much the same thing. Governing itself by rule, objectivity tries methodically to eliminate bias, prejudice, and all the distortions that go by the name of subjectivity. This Cartesian endeavor assumes that a methodically purified consciousness guarantees certainty. On one level, objectivity consists in humble self-effacement, but on another, it is marked by a distinct arrogance insofar as it makes individual self-consciousness the locus and arbiter of truth. Though it is by definition not subjective, then, objectivity as an ideal derives from a highly subjectivist epistemology.

This epistemology can explain how objective interpretation is possible but not why it is ever necessary. Why is it ever more than a matter of convenience or curiosity to understand another's mind if one's own is the sufficient condition of truth? If we acknowledge the subversion of the authority of reflexive consciousness accomplished by Nietzsche, Marx, and Freud, or if, like Gadamer, we agree with Heidegger than consciousness always *is* more than it knows, then this more that it is cannot be understood by trusting solely to the self-governance of consciousness. In Gadamer's view, interpretation of tradition is capable, where introspection is not, of understanding the truth that exceeds self-consciousness—exceeds it because, however conscientious, consciousness belongs to historical tradition. Consciousness cannot, by pulling on the bootstraps of method, extricate itself from the very history of which it is a part. If there is indeed a truth that exceeds what can be methodologically certified, its disclosure invariably requires an interpretation of tradition from within tradition, which interpretation (being circular) cannot be called objective, although it is not necessarily subjective either.

Instead of seeing interpretation as an objective or subjective act, Gadamer thinks of it as playing a game. In playing, we do not stand over against the game; we participate in it. A player who does not get fully involved in the game is called a spoilsport, because toying with or playing at a game spoils it. By contrast, taking a game seriously entails belonging to it, and this belonging in turn precludes treating the game as an object. Moreover, in the same process of playing that prevents objectifying the game, players lose their status as subjects. As part of the game, participants play parts that are not merely themselves insofar as they have been assigned roles to perform. Playing consists in a performance of what is no object, by what is no subject. And if interpreting is like playing, as Gadamer argues, then it always involves something like performing a drama, for the player who takes the play seriously interprets it from within, by belonging to and playing a part in it.

The larger drama in which we cannot choose not to play is history. Human being exists historically; therefore, interpreting historical tradition from within requires no prior specification of rules because such interpretation cannot be avoided, and it is in fact the condition of methodologism itself. To assert the contrary—to say that at some point interpretation of tradition is unnecessary—is to assert that at some point consciousness is nonhistorical and self-grounding. But if this Cartesian thesis is mistaken, it follows that all interpretation of tradition (as of everything else) occurs within tradition. Negatively put, there is no presuppositionless, nontraditional interpretation. Rather, understanding always begins within and returns to an already given horizon of understanding.

The hermeneutical circle is distinct from linear induction because not only do the parts lead to an understanding of the whole but there must also be an understanding of the whole prior to any examination of the parts. This prior understanding of the whole Gadamer calls a prejudice, a judgment that precedes inquiry. The necessity of such pre-judgment indicates that understanding is always possible only insofar as understanding has already begun. To understand tradition from within tradition means to be prejudiced. But if prejudice is the condition of interpretation and true interpretation is nevertheless possible, then though not all prejudices are true, they are not all ipso facto false either. The function of conscientious interpretation is not to eradicate all prejudices but rather to sort out the true ones from the false; and this discrimination cannot be performed at the outset, by an act of will, but only in the very process of projection and ad hoc revision that is interpretation itself.

A true interpretation, in Gadamer's opinion, is one that has performed this discrimination of false from true prejudices, the latter being those confirmed by the text. True interpretation nevertheless remains within the horizon of prejudice that is the interpreter's world. That world horizon is not fixed and immutable, however, like a circle in which the interpreter is forever circumscribed: the horizon of understanding, no less than the visual horizon, can change. Gadamer images the process by which the interpreter's horizon is broadened as a dialectical fusion of horizons—a dialogue in which the text puts questions to the interpreter even as the interpreter puts questions to the text. This dialogue is always possible because both the author of the text and the interpreter of it speak a language, whether or not they speak the same one. For the interpreter as well as the author, to understand is to find a language to express that understanding. Interpreting, like translation, consists in finding, within the resources of the interpreter's language, a common language that can say both what the text means and what the interpreter understands of it. As the fusion of languages, interpretation is the process by which one's own horizon of language is fused with that of another and thereby expanded. In dialogue, a common language is formed that makes understanding possible. For this reason, language itself cannot be objectified. We can and do understand our language, of course, but we understand what is said and not the language per se. Language is always presupposed by objectification; it cannot be made an object precisely because it is itself the condition of objectification. Beyond the sphere of objectivity and including it, Gadamer writes, "Being that can be understood is language" (*Truth and Method*, 474). The scope of hermeneutic understanding is coextensive with that of being.

Gadamer's argument for the universality of hermeneutics implies that there can be no critique of tradition that is not itself traditional, no falsification of another's opinion that does not presuppose a common language in which the dispute is carried out. All thought depends on a dialogically reached consensus that cannot be called into question as a whole since it is only against this background that questions make sense. But Gadamer is tempted to equate tradition, this common ground, with truth. To avoid such a tacit legitimation of the status quo Jürgen Habermas stresses an element of dialogue that Gadamer slights: its critical, emancipating interest. Gadamer assumes, according to Habermas, that every apparent dialogue is real, ignoring the possibility that the participants may be "talking past each other" without realizing it. Such pseudo-communication will result in an illusory consensus, and no further dialogue will of itself be able to dispel that illusion. Moreover, a consensus that has apparently been reached in free dialogue may actually have been enforced by implicit forms of coercion and domination that are quite unknown to the speakers. This coercion will be least recognizable, in fact, when the forms of domination are woven into the very language that to all appearances unites the parties in unfettered debate. Insofar as language itself is a form of sedimented violence, systematically distorted communication cannot be recognized and rectified while participating in it. Rather, only a nonparticipating, external observer can provide correct diagnosis and appropriate therapy.

Habermas suggests the psychoanalyst on the individual level and the critic of ideology on the societal level as examples of observers who operate at the limit of hermeneutic universality, where dialogic understanding does not suffice. "The 'what,' the meaning-content of systematically distorted expressions, can only be 'understood' when it is possible to answer, at the same time, the 'why' questions, i.e., to 'explain' the emergence of the symptomatic scene by reference to the initial conditions of the systematic distortion itself" ("Hermeneutic Claim," 194). Extrapolating the borderline, hermeneutic-explanatory task of the psychoanalyst to the "hidden pathology of societal systems" involves the assumption that "every consensus, as the outcome of an understanding of meaning, is, in principle, suspect of having been enforced through pseudo-communication" (205). The critique of ideology involves a principled suspicion of tradition such as that given voice by the Enlightenment, a recognition that not every actual consensus is the locus of truth. For this reason, each actual consensus must be evaluated in the light of a regulative ideal "according to which truth would only be guaranteed by *that* kind of consensus which is achieved under the idealized conditions of unlimited communication free from domination and could be maintained over time" (205). This regulative ideal is the methodological correlative of the emancipatory interest implicit in all dialogue, a utopian impulse not just to understand reality but to change it for the better.

Whereas Gadamer, believing that language cannot finally be objectified, has little interest in the specifics of modern linguistics or philosophy of language, Habermas does not hesitate to borrow from the insights of Peircean semiotics and the linguistics of Chomsky and Piaget. Precisely insofar as any language can itself be a mode of repression, merely understanding, speaking, and listening to it cannot lead to emancipation. Instead, the analyst also needs to be able to explain the language's systematic functioning; and it is at this point, where understanding alone falls short, that the objectification performed by linguistics becomes necessary.

Structural linguistics in particular has come to be seen not merely as a supplement or alternative to hermeneutics but as its antithesis; and although this is not the place to elaborate on the antihermeneutic impetus of the 1960s and 1970s, it must at least be mentioned in even so brief a survey as this. "Linguistics is not hermeneutic,"

Jonathan Culler asserts. "It does not discover what a sequence means or produce a new interpretation of it but tries to determine the nature of the system underlying the [speech] event" (*Structuralist Poetics*, 31). The application of Saussurean linguistics to literary study promoted poetics rather than hermeneutics; and as structural poetics came to dominate the field of literature, the result was not just an avoidance of interpretation but a positive animus against it. "There are many tasks that confront criticism," Culler contends, "many things we need to advance our understanding of literature, but one thing we do not need is more interpretation of literary works" (*Pursuit of Signs*, 6).

Such statements are in part a reaction to the tedious proliferation of New Critical "readings" in the 1950s and 1960s. But over and above indictments of formalist explication de texte, interpretation came under broader and more developed attack from deconstruction. Deconstructive analysis goes beyond demonstrating the impossibility of univocally decoding the secret of a text to suggest, in Jacques Derrida's words, "the possibility that indeed it might have no secret, that it might only be pretending to be simulating some hidden truth within its folds" (*Spurs*, 133). Of Nietzschean deconstruction Derrida writes, "The hermeneutic project which postulates a true sense of the text is disqualified under this regime. Reading is freed from the horizon of meaning or truth of being, liberated from the values of the product's production or the present's presence. . . . Truth in the guise of production, the unveiling/dissimulation of the present product, is dismantled. The veil [is] no more raised than it is lowered" (107).

As the archetypal metaphor of interpretation, the unveiling of meaning and truth that Derrida here repudiates is an image as ancient as hermeneutics itself. It appears as early as the Pseudo-Areopagite, in the fourth century, and as late as Heidegger. In a crucial passage of his "Defense of Poetry," however, Shelley juxtaposes unveiling with another, and no less primordial, image of interpretation: "Veil after veil may be undrawn [from the poem], and the inmost naked beauty of the meaning never exposed. A great poem is a fountain forever overflowing with the waters of wisdom and delight; and after one person and one age has exhausted all its divine effluence which their peculiar relations enable them to share, another and yet another succeeds, and new relations are ever developed, the source of an unforeseen and unconceived delight" (509). Though Shelley draws no distinction between unveiling and overflowing, since both figure the inexhaustibility of interpretation, there is an evident tension between the two images. As unveiling, interpretation descends from surface to depth: it penetrates the superficial to reach the profound. Because it must lift or rend a concealing veil, such interpretation construes its object as an inmost nakedness, an inner kernel, or a dark secret. The project of interpretive unveiling images the true as the hidden. Overflow, by contrast, ascends from depth to surface. As figured in the image of the fountain, interpretation is the poem's continuing emergence, exposition, or exteriorization. Interpretive overflow figures the true as the apparent.

No one has explicated, or integrated, these conflicting models of interpretation better than Paul Ricoeur, and with his work I will conclude this overview. Throughout Ricoeur's work, whatever the immediate topic, two distinct moments—of doubt, and of faith— can be discerned. The energy of his thought derives largely from his resisting the temptation to resign these moments to antithesis, to juxtapose them in a facile eclecticism, or, worst of all, to let one eclipse the other.

The names Ricoeur gives the two moments vary with the occasion. Best known, "the hermeneutics of suspicion" refers to the necessary task of unveiling, of doubt. It involves the suspicion, as Horkheimer once brutally remarked, that the edifice of culture is built on dogshit. The hermeneutics of suspicion comprehends not only critique of ideology, orthodox Marxist philosophy, and Freudian psychoanalysis but also Husserl's eidetic reduction and some aspects of structural linguistics and anthropology. Common to these modes of skeptical interpretation is the suspicion (amounting to a deeply held belief) that all forms of consciousness and tradition conceal something to which the knowing, speaking subject is not privy and which therefore necessitates an objective interpretation that the subject has no authority to confirm or to deny.

Ricoeur suspects, however, that the hermeneutics of suspicion is itself only a half-truth. The bloom is no less real than the manure it feeds on. Ricoeur associates Hegel, Heidegger, Bultmann, and Gadamer with a faith that is not merely naive, because it in fact points up the naiveté of mere suspicion. This is the faith that a pre-objective understanding, a shared community, precedes, grounds, and limits all subsequent activities of objectification. All interpretation is the continuing development, the overflow of fullness, from that primordial unity.

Addressing himself to Lévi-Strauss, Ricoeur asks, "Can the structuralist explanation . . . be separated from *all* hermeneutic comprehension?" (*Conflict of Interpretations*, 55). He responds that there can be "no structural analysis . . . without hermeneutic comprehension of the transfer of sense (without 'metaphor,' without *translatio*), without that indirect giving of meaning which founds the semantic field, which in turn provides the ground upon which structural homologies can be discerned" (60). Ricoeur similarly asks of Habermas the hermeneutical question, "From where do you speak when you appeal to *Selbstreflexion*, if it is not from the place that you yourself have denounced as a non-place? . . . It is indeed from the basis of a tradition that you speak. This tradition is not perhaps the same as Gadamer's. . . . But it is a tradition nonetheless, the tradition of emancipation rather than that of recollection. Critique is also a tradition" (*Hermeneutics and the Human Sciences*, 99).

Yet despite his critique of Lévi-Strauss and Habermas, Ricoeur scarcely abandons the structural, critical, or objective moment of interpretation, for this is precisely the standard by which he criticizes Bultmann:

> Even if it is true, finally, that the text accomplishes its meaning only in personal appropriation (and this I believe strongly with Bultmann against all the current philosophies of a discourse without the subject), this appropriation is only the final state, the last threshold of an understanding which has been first uprooted and moved into another meaning. The moment of exegesis is not that of existential decision but that of "meaning," which, as Frege and Husserl [and Betti] have said, is an objective and even "ideal" moment. . .
>
> The semantic moment, the moment of objective meaning, must precede the existential moment, the moment of personal decision, in a hermeneutics concerned with doing justice to both the objectivity of meaning and the historicity of personal decision. In this respect the problem Bultmann posed is the exact inverse of the problem which contemporary structuralist theories pose. The structuralist theories have taken the "language" side, whereas Bultmann has taken the "speaking" side. But we now need an instrument of thought for apprehending the connection between language and speaking, the conversion of system into event. [*Conflict of Interpretations*, 397]

Ricoeur's ambition has been to locate the site of this conversion, the multidimensional intersection of langue and parole, structure and history, consensus and creativity, objectivity and subjectivity, fact and value, explanation and understanding, distanciation and appropriation, doubt and faith. In *Freud and Philosophy*, his most intensive meditation on this topic, Ricoeur identifies the symbol as the locus of this intersection:

> The thesis I am proposing is this: what psychoanalysis calls overdetermination cannot be understood apart from a dialectic between two functions which are thought to be opposed to one

another but which symbols coordinate in a concrete unity. Thus the ambiguity of symbolism is not a lack of univocity but is rather the possibility of carrying and engendering opposed interpretations, each of which is self-consistent.

The two hermeneutics, one turned toward the revival of archaic meanings belonging to the infancy of mankind, the other toward the emergence of figures that anticipate our spiritual adventure, develop, in opposite directions, the beginnings of meaning contained in language—a language richly endowed with the enigmas that men have invented and received in order to express their fears and hopes. Thus we should say that symbols carry two vectors. On the one hand, symbols repeat our childhood in all the senses, chronological and nonchronological, of that childhood. On the other hand, they explore our adult life; "O my prophetic soul," says Hamlet. But these two functions are not external to one another; they constitute the overdetermination of authentic symbols. . . . These authentic symbols are truly regressive-progressive; remembrance gives rise to anticipation; archaism gives rise to prophecy. [282]

Such symbols lend themselves to an archaeological hermeneutics that searches out origins, the subliminal beginnings of subjectivity in a systematic economics of desire that can be studied objectively. But authentic symbols also lend themselves to a teleological hermeneutics that looks not to the primitive past but to a supraliminal future beyond objectivity. Teleological hermeneutics is not objective, because it has no object. It discloses no dark secret and conceals none, because it does not discover an underlying system; instead it participates in a continuing genesis of meaning, a history where meaning derives from successive rather than simultaneous differences. If in archaeological hermeneutics interpreting the symbol consists in retrospection on its repressed past, in teleological hermeneutics the symbol's meaning depends prospectively on a released future, on what the symbol will come to mean in the continuing history of its interpretation. In the overdetermined symbol these two hermeneutics converge: "Authentic symbols are truly regressive-progressive" as Ricoeur writes. Their remembrance of the archaic past precludes naive faith, while their prophetic anticipation of the future precludes naive doubt. In interpreting the symbol, the twin moments of descent and ascent, skepticism and hope, are one.

There is no reason to suppose that the history of hermeneutics comes to a conclusion, or even a climax, in Ricoeur's dialectical mediation of the conflict of interpretations. His own thought is still in the process of development, still open to the future, as is hermeneutics itself. Yet Ricoeur's work offers an appropriate conclusion for this brief survey. Modern hermeneutics, like the individual fields of interpretation it comprehends, is rife with struggle between opposed positions, each claiming to subvert or supersede the others. Ricoeur's great merit lies in his refusal to minimize any of his predecessors' genuinely valuable contributions to hermeneutics, no matter how irreconcilable they appear. He tries to integrate when he can; but when he cannot, Ricoeur re-creates within himself, as it were, the conflict of interpretations that is modern hermeneutics.

2

WHAT IS PHILOSOPHICAL

ABOUT PHILOSOPHICAL

HERMENEUTICS?

In a 1965 review of *Truth and Method*, virtually the first introduction of Gadamer to an American audience, E. D. Hirsch observed, "If we cannot enunciate a principle for distinguishing between an interpretation that is valid and one that is not, there is little point in writing books about texts or about hermeneutic theory."[1] Even conceding that such a principle of interpretive validity could be formulated, one would have to agree with Hirsch that Gadamer offers none. I would admit still further that Gadamer's hermeneutics has no practical applications, no consequences that would improve the practice of literary criticism. But I argue that this inapplicability implies no indictment. The impracticality of *Truth and Method* stems directly from the kind of book it is and from the substance of its theses; and now, more than two decades after Hirsch's influential review, when the "against theory" movement is

1. Reprinted in appendix II of Hirsch, *Validity in Interpretation*, 251. Some scholars have noted that in this review Hirsch does not state Gadamer's position accurately. See, e.g., Bagwell, *American Formalism and the Problem of Interpretation*, 108n.

gaining momentum even among theorists, it seems possible to give Gadamer's position a more sympathetic hearing.

A hermeneutic theory that establishes no principle of validity may well be pointless and inconsequential, but this charge, even if it is true, leaves Gadamer's philosophical hermeneutics untouched. "The purpose of my investigation," Gadamer bluntly states, "is not to offer a general theory of interpretation" (*Truth and Method*, xxxi).[2] If this self-assessment is correct, the lack of practical applicability shows not that philosophical hermeneutics is pointless but only that it is not a theory. No single fact is more crucial than this to an understanding of *Truth and Method*, for to distinguish philosophy from theory is to open up the fundamental question of what makes philosophical hermeneutics specifically philosophical.

If Gadamer's account of interpretation is not a theory, then what is? "Theory" has many meanings, of course, but here we need be concerned only with its meaning in the limited context of hermeneutics and literary criticism. Josef Bleicher distinguishes three varieties of contemporary hermeneutics: hermeneutic theory as represented by Betti, hermeneutic philosophy as expounded by Gadamer, and critical hermeneutics as exemplified by Habermas. The first of these Bleicher defines as follows:

> *Hermeneutic theory* focuses on the problematic of a general theory of interpretation as the methodology for the human sciences. . . . Through the analysis of *verstehen* as the method appropriate to the re-experiencing or re-thinking of what an author had originally felt or thought, Betti hoped to gain an insight into the process of understanding in general. . . . The methodologically developed use of our intuitive capacity serves the acquisition of "relatively objective" knowledge. It ap-

2. The foreword to the second edition (1965), in which this statement is found, appeared in the same year as Hirsch's review of the first edition. Thus he had no access to it.

proaches "meaning-full forms" with a set of "canons" which have been formulated in order to facilitate the correct interpretation of . . . human expressions. [*Contemporary Hermeneutics*, 1–2]

In emphasizing the relation between theory and method, Bleicher's definition accords with that of Steven Knapp and Walter Benn Michaels in their landmark essay, "Against Theory": "By 'theory' we mean . . . the attempt to govern interpretations of particular texts by appealing to an account of interpretation in general" (723). Theory, thus defined, is the foundation of methodology; it is inherently practical insofar as it entails the construction of general principles whose very purpose is to govern interpretive practice.

Further specifying the nature of hermeneutic theory, Hirsch observes that it "has always recognized that there may be different kinds of textual interpretation corresponding to different kinds of texts. . . . Emilio Betti . . . perceives three main types: re-cognitive, presentational, and normative, corresponding respectively to historical and literary texts, dramatic and musical texts, and legal and sacred texts" (*Validity in Interpretation*, 112). From this irreducible plurality follows a universal principle basic to hermeneutic theory,[3] namely, that there is no universal method of interpretation, only the various methods relative to particular types of interpretable texts.

With this concept of hermeneutic theory in mind, we are better prepared to understand what Gadamer's purpose is and is not: "The purpose of my investigation is not to offer a general theory of interpretation and a differential account of its methods (which Emi-

---

3. I consider Hirsch a theorist, though he has disavowed that label ("Against Theory?" 48–52). First, his claim that "critical practice is what we choose to make it" (52) is a quintessentially *theoretical* claim—one which, as I show below, Gadamer denies. Second, Hirsch's well-known principle, which Gadamer likewise denies, that understanding precedes application, that theoria precedes praxis, is no less fundamentally a *theoretical* principle.

lio Betti had done so well) but to discover what is common to all modes of understanding" (*Truth and Method,* xxxi). The fact that Gadamer's aim is to reveal what is common to understanding makes his hermeneutics a general account of interpretation, to be sure; but this generality does not make it theoretical, because it lacks the other ingredient essential to theory: the attempt to establish regulative principles and thereby govern interpretation. On this point Gadamer is quite specific: "I did not wish to elaborate a system of rules to describe, let alone direct, the methodical procedure of the human sciences" (xxviii). Unlike the theorist Betti, Gadamer makes no attempt to differentiate the distinctive methods of the several kinds of interpretation: he is intent on what is common to them all. Gadamer certainly does not dispute the conclusion, typical of hermeneutic theory, that no universal method governs interpretation. Quite the contrary, he takes it as evidence for his own inference that what is universal to understanding is not a method. This thesis has far-reaching philosophical implications, for if not all understanding is governed by method, then theoretical methodology does not exclusively determine which interpretations are true.[4] Simply put, method does not exhaust truth. That is the central thesis of *Truth and Method.*

These considerations should make it clearer why Gadamer's hermeneutics lacks practical implications. As he himself explained, "[It was not] my aim to investigate the theoretical foundations of work in [the human sciences] in order to put my findings to practical ends" (xxviii). Such an aim would have been nonsensical in view of the fact that Gadamer offers no theory and therefore does not and cannot make proposals for regulating interpretive practice. His thesis is indeed that understanding understanding does not depend on elaborating a principle of validity in interpretation, for interpretive prac-

4. Methodology does determine validity, however, precisely insofar as validity is defined as an inference generated by method.

tice does not ultimately consist in the application of principles based on interpretive theories. Gadamer's hermeneutics is philosophical in intent: not only does it have no practical applications but, further, any attempt to put it into practice constitutes a misinterpretation of it.

On "the question of whether metaphysics offers anything of practical utility to hermeneutic theory," Hirsch answers in the negative. "Heideggerian metaphysics," he writes, is powerless to dictate what ought to be chosen in the realm of values" (*Aims of Interpretation*, 84–85).[5] But no more than Hirsch or Heidegger himself is Gadamer under any illusions on this question. "For Heidegger," Gadamer states, "the existential analytic of Dasein implies no particular historical ideal of existence" (*Truth and Method*, 262). Gadamer derives no interpretive ideal from Heidegger; and though interpretive ethics is not his focus, when he does consider the matter, his conclusions on the issue of prejudice coincide exactly with those of Hirsch and every other responsible interpreter. "There is undoubtedly no understanding that is free of all prejudices," he states, "however much the will of our knowledge must be directed towards escaping their thrall" (490). That we always need to break the bonds of prejudice because we are always bound by them is a maxim of interpretive ethics that Gadamer nowhere denies and indeed here affirms.

Isn't escaping prejudice, however, precisely the aim of method? It is true, Gadamer writes, that "the methods of the human sciences are not at issue" in *Truth and Method*; but he goes on to say, "I did not remotely intend to deny the necessity of methodical work within the human sciences" (xxviii–xxix). This affirmation need not be read as disingenuous or merely concessive, for Gadamer has no quarrel with method except in one particular: the claim that method has a monopoly on truth. Gadamer wholeheartedly affirms the need for me-

5. For a critique of Hirsch's reliance on an ethics of interpretation from a scholar on the right, see Juhl, *Interpretation*.

thodical work, denying only that method is all we need. "The legal historian," he notes, "has his 'methods' of avoiding mistakes, and in such matters I agree entirely with the legal historian."

"But the hermeneutic interest of the philosopher," Gadamer continues, "begins precisely when error has been successfully avoided" (xxxiii). In our context, this means Gadamer's hermeneutic *philosophy* begins just at the point where hermeneutic *theory* ends. In principle, hermeneutic theory offers legitimate methods, which interpreters ought to and can apply in order to avoid errors. The question, then, is whether there is any purpose for philosophy once theoretical methodology has done its work and enabled us to prevent mistakes. This is precisely the question of whether truth is exhausted by method, and Gadamer answers it in the negative. That method is in fact limited, that understanding exceeds the realm of certainty and error governed by method, that true interpretation cannot be exhaustively methodized, and that truth therefore exceeds method—all of these insights lie at the heart of *Truth and Method*.

The book provides its own defense—that is, a defense of hermeneutic philosophy, which stakes its claim on the far side of the limit, beyond theory and the methods it grounds. Hermeneutic philosophy requires such a defense insofar as hermeneutic theory would proclaim its own universality, asserting that there is no far side of method and thus that hermeneutic philosophy has no subject matter and no raison d'être. The rationale of theory, in contrast, is to govern interpretive practice; for that reason, theory is characterized by a constitutive suspicion of interpretation, since it conceives interpretive practice as intrinsically deficient and in need of theoretical regulation. It is therefore no accident that the proliferation of an animus against interpretation has coincided very closely with the rise of theory.[6] Here, then, is the essential conflict between herme-

6. Now, it seems, the pendulum is swinging back. The movement that began, say, with Susan Sontag's "Against Interpretation" (1965) is now ending with Knapp and Michaels's "Against Theory." As Stanley Fish observes, "Theory's day is dying" (Mitchell, *Against Theory*, p. 128).

neutic theory and hermeneutic philosophy, for Gadamer contends that not hermeneutic theory but hermeneutics—interpretation itself—is universal in scope (*Philosophical Hermeneutics*, 3–43). The self-defense of hermeneutic philosophy is also a defense of interpretation against theory.

Gadamer's purpose, as he describes it, is "to discover what is common to all modes of understanding" (*Truth and Method*, xxxi). This common factor, shared alike by literary, historical, legal, and scriptural interpretation, is that no type of interpretation is susceptible of being exhaustively programmed. Just as hermeneutic theory concludes that there is no universal canon of interpretive regulations but only local rules relative to particular genres, Gadamer's hermeneutic philosophy concludes that what is universal to interpretation, if there is anything universal at all, is not a canon of interpretive regulations. But it seems, then, that hermeneutic philosophy has as its subject matter only a negative universal, a shared lack—rather like saying that what is common to all kinds of fruit is that none can be manufactured. Such a conclusion, even if true, is of little use to *homo fabricans*.

It is, after all, primarily in industry, or more generally in technology, that theories find practical application. Even if students of literature are repulsed by the notion of an interpretation industry, many still tacitly cherish the notion that the ideal interpretation is that which is the product of and is legitimated by applied theory; and this suggests that interpretation ideally consists of controlled production, of subjectively regulated creation. Insofar as the very purpose of literary or any other theory is to govern practice, Gadamer is quite right to state, "Modern theory is a tool of construction by means of which we gather experiences in a unified way and make it possible to dominate them" (454). Offering dominion over literary experience, interpretation controlled by applied theory is a function of the will to power.

Hermeneutic theory shows interpreters how they do or must act in order to achieve the end of validity. Not only do theorists construct theories; their theories enable interpreters in turn to construct objective interpretations. This whole process, in Gadamer's words, "is dominated by the idea of construction" (454). Whether normative or descriptive, whether a theory prescribes how interpretations ought to be made or describes how they are in fact made, the basic presumption of hermeneutic theory is, simply, that interpretations are made: interpreting is something interpreters do, an act of *construere*, of construal or construction, which can be regulated and should be.

To a certain extent this is no doubt true. But if hermeneutic theory exhausts the sphere of what interpreters do and ought to do, the question again confronts us: What is left for hermeneutic philosophy? Like Dilthey, Gadamer takes up the challenge of writing a critique of historical reason, one that would in certain respects parallel Kant's *Critique of Pure Reason*. That *Truth and Method* is philosophy does not mean it deduces from principles how historical interpretation must change in order to achieve philosophical legitimacy. Gadamer writes,

> Kant certainly did not intend to prescribe what modern science must do in order to stand honorably before the judgment seat of reason. He asked a *philosophical* question: what are the conditions of our knowledge by virtue of which modern science is possible, and how far does it extend? The following investigation also asks a philosophic question. . . . It asks (to put it in Kantian terms): How is understanding possible? This is a question which precedes any action of understanding on the part of subjectivity, including the methodical activity of the "interpretive sciences" and their norms and rules. [xxix–xxx; italics added]

Gadamer directs his inquiry toward what precedes the activity of regulated understanding and even the activity of unregulated understanding, for the philosophical question is, What precedes any act of understanding on our part and makes it possible? We can agree that whatever makes understanding possible will be universal to all interpretation; but it is puzzling, to say the least, that Gadamer locates what all interpreters share in something that is prior to any interpretive act. Precisely this, however, is the locus of hermeneutic philosophy. As Gadamer says, "The purpose of my investigation is . . . to discover what is common to all modes of understanding and to show that understanding is never a subjective relation to a given object" (xxxi). The universal element of understanding, then, is not some behavior or activity common to all interpreters, for from a philosophical standpoint understanding is not construal or construction, not the act of a subject on an object; it is not fundamentally something interpreters do at all. From the standpoint of hermeneutic theory, of course, that is all interpretation is; and even if theory exhausts the sphere of what interpreters do and should do, it still has not sighted the domain of hermeneutic philosophy on the far side of the limit, beyond the act of interpretation. Hermeneutic philosophy has no practical applications, and can have none, precisely because it is not concerned with what interpreters do.

"My real concern," Gadamer asserts, "was and is *philosophic*: not what we do or what we ought to do, but what happens to us over and above our wanting and doing" (xxviii; italics added). That philosophical hermeneutics has nothing to offer the interpretation industry is no mere deficiency; and although it does not concern itself with interpretive acts, it does not have for its subject matter a merely negative universal. Gadamer's topic is not what we do but what happens to us. His subject is what befalls us beyond what we do or want to do, beyond the will to power, and beyond methodological control. *Truth and Method* cannot be applied to practice because it is concerned with an event that happens universally to interpreters, one we can do nothing about. What is universal to hermeneutics is necessarily inevitable as well. If the realm of theory—which comprehends what we can and should do—is limited, beyond that limit there is, in truth, nothing to be done.

Under these circumstances, isn't the danger of hermeneutic philosophy that the very impossibility of practical *applications* will engender practical *effects* of the worst kind, namely, demoralization and defeatism, the capitulation of lazy reason resulting from the discovery that something happens to us in interpreting that eludes our control? Method is a form of self-induced necessity, the free self-determinism of reason; and because method is an expression of reason's freedom, reason balks at the idea that method is not absolute, that there is any determinism beyond its own. No doubt there appears to be an element of fatalism in Gadamer's hermeneutic philosophy, as in every attempt to discern the limit of freedom, reason, and will. That there is such a limit, however, we learn from tragedy, for here the power of will confronts the power of what exceeds it, which we call fate. We might look to tragedy, therefore, to discover the possible effects of hermeneutic philosophy, since both suggest there is nothing to be done.

Tragedy too has no practical applications—there is something evidently absurd about trying to apply *Oedipus Rex* to one's daily life—but its effects are real enough. Pity and fear can be considered debilitating emotions of the same kind that hermeneutic philosophy may be charged with evoking. Yet Aristotle says that tragedy also effects a catharsis of them. In viewing a tragic drama, Gadamer explains, "There is a disjunction from what is happening, a refusal to accept . . . the agonizing events. But the effect of the tragic catastrophe is precisely to dissolve this disjunction from what is." The cathartic effect proceeds from affirmation as well as resignation.

> But what is the real object of this affirmation? . . . The excess of tragic consequences is characteristic of the essence of the tragic. Despite all the subjectivization of guilt in modern tragedy, it still retains an element of the classical sense of the power of destiny

that, in the very disproportion between guilt and fate, reveals itself as the same for all. . . . So we must repeat the question: what does the spectator affirm here? Obviously it is the disproportionate, terrible immensity of the consequences that flow from a guilty deed that is the real claim made on the spectator. The tragic affirmation is the fulfillment of this claim. It has the character of a genuine communion. What is experienced in such an excess of tragic suffering is something truly common. The spectator recognizes himself and his own finiteness in the face of the power of fate. What happens to the great ones of the earth has an exemplary significance. Tragic pensiveness does not affirm the tragic course of events as such, or the justice of the fate that overtakes the hero but rather a metaphysical order of being that is true for all. To see that "this is how it is" is a kind of self-knowledge for the spectator, who emerges with new insight from the illusions in which he, like everyone else, lives [131–32]

More than justice or punishment, the catastrophe exceeds the hero's just deserts. "I am a man more sinned against than sinning," Lear cries. The disproportion between guilt and fate, between what he does and what happens to him, is the tragedy; and it demands of the spectator not only acceptance but affirmation. The metaphysical truth affirmed by tragedy and by Gadamer as "truly common" and "true for all" is that human beings do not manage their destinies. When Gadamer describes his purpose as discovering "what is common to all modes of understanding," the discovery he envisions does not just pertain to understanding but is the universal truth of human being. This truth is something we can do nothing about. It derives not from proof or intersubjective agreement. Rather we learn it from tragedy, from being confronted with the littleness of knowing, feeling, intending, doing—the littleness of all subjective acts in the face of what happens. Overriding our hopes and intentions, the universal truth can be learned only through suffering. As Aeschylus expresses it, *pathei mathos*. "What a man has to learn through suffering," Gadamer explains, "is not this or that particular thing, but insight into the limitations of humanity, into the absoluteness of the barrier that separates man from the divine" (557). The finitude of human being consists simply in the fact that events happen beyond anyone's control. Tragedy discloses the unmanageable effects of such events; it affirms the effect of history on subjectivity as what is true for all, and it is therefore true of understanding as well. Thus Gadamer writes, "The purpose of my investigation is . . . to discover what is common to all modes of understanding and to show that understanding is never a subjective relation to a given object but to the history of its effect" (xxxi).

Considered in relation to history, interpretation is not the act of an interpreting subject on an interpretable object. Of course, we do say (in subject-object syntax) "I question this" and "I doubt that." But we also say "a question arises" and "a doubt occurs to me." Similarly, Gadamer inquires not into the "I interpret it" but instead into the "an interpretation occurs to me." When insight occurs to us, it is then that we understand. As a flash of enlightenment, the epiphany of understanding is not something we do but something that happens to us. It is an effect of history. Thus hermeneutic philosophy considers understanding not as subjective behavior but as a response to effective-history.

In the light of tragedy, to understand is not to do but to suffer, to be overwhelmed by the course of events. Yet the effect of a genuinely tragic course of events is not only pity and fear but insight as well. In watching a tragedy, the insight occurs to us that common to all understanding is its being an effect of tragic history. Then we truly see that what is common to all is common to us, for our seeing is itself an effect of being overwhelmed by the tragic course of events, that is, sharing in the fate of hero and spectator alike.

This seeing that results from sharing is of particular importance to Gadamer, and it bears further consideration. Spectators, we usually say, are nonparticipants: they have no share in the events. If we recall that the Greek word *theorein* means "seeing," "spectation," it becomes clearer how the English word "theory" could be opposed to practice. This is not to suggest that the spectator of tragedy is a theorist, however. Quite the opposite, Gadamer says, the spectator is more like the Greek *theoros*, for whom

> watching something is a genuine mode of participation. Here we can recall the concept of sacral communion that lies behind the original Greek concept of theoria. Theoros means someone who takes part in a delegation to a festival. Such a person has no other distinction or function than to be there. Thus the theoros is a spectator in the proper sense of the word, since he participates in the solemn act through his presence at it. . . . Theoria is a true participation, not something active but something passive (pathos), namely being totally involved in and carried away by what one sees. [124–25][7]

The theoros or spectator is involved in a way that is not an action but a pathos. Spectators not only watch the performance but suffer what is performed on them, a pathos, rather than their own deeds. Moreover, their seeing is won by sharing, for as the spectators watch, they are caught up in the tragic course of events; and it is precisely by passively taking part in the tragic history that the spectators see and understand. By sharing, the theoros comes to an insight denied the theorist: the insight that participating in the tragedy is not a matter of choice. If tragedy discloses the universal impact of history on finite beings, then pathei mathos means there is no knower of history that is not also a participant in history, no theory of history that is not also involved in historical practice, and

---

7. In this passage, Gadamer is expanding on Heidegger's related remarks in *Being and Time*, 98–99. Richard Bernstein, too, identifies the happening of understanding with pathos in "From Hermeneutics to Praxis," 91.

hence no pure theory of history at all. Positively stated, given the ultimate unity of theory and practice, all understanding of history is an effect of history. This effect is not the result of a force operating on us from without. All understanding occurs to us because we belong to history.

Belonging to history is Gadamer's way of describing a fact that is apparent to everyone. With sufficient historical training, we can always determine when something was written, even without knowing who wrote it. In replying to Betti, Gadamer explains,

> For example, when you read a classic essay by Mommsen you immediately know its era, the only era when it could have been written. Even a master of the historical method is not able to keep himself entirely free from the prejudices of his time, his social environment, and his natural situation, etc. Is this a failing? And even if it were, I regard it as a necessary philosophical task to consider why this failure always occurs wherever anything is achieved. In other words, I consider the only scientific thing is *to recognize what is* . . . and to envisage in a fundamentally universal way what *always* happens. [512][8]

The *philosophical* task is to discern what always happens—that is, what is common to all modes of understanding; and what is common to them is that even the most objective interpretation betrays when it was written by registering the impact of then current social, intellectual, and political forces.

The effect of history is manifest in every interpretation—or rather in every interpretation but our own. This exception may mean that the force of history has now been finally controlled by methodologi-

8. A basic issue in the dispute between Gadamer and Betti is whether one can determine the possibility of understanding without also determining the possibility of true understanding. Lawrence Hinman answers in the negative, and so sides with Betti, in "Quid Facti or Quid Juris." See also Apel, *Towards a Transformation of Philosophy.*

cal safeguards conducive to objectivity. Gadamer concludes, however, that, quite the opposite, the transparency of our times to us is not the exception but the universal rule, for all responsible interpreters consider themselves to be telling the eternal truth. History is always invisible to the participants in it; and for this reason methodological prophylactics, however necessary, always ultimately fail. To dispel the illusion of our immunity from history is the effect not only of tragedy but of Gadamer's hermeneutics also. "If there is any practical consequence of the present investigation," Gadamer asserts in *Truth and Method*, "it certainly has nothing to do with an unscientific 'commitment'; instead, it is concerned with the 'scientific' integrity of acknowledging the commitment involved in all understanding" (xxviii). Furthermore, "These consequences do not need to be such that a theory is applied to practice so that the latter is performed differently, i.e. in a way that is technically correct. They could also consist in correcting (and refining) . . . the way in which constantly exercised understanding understands itself" (266).

The change Gadamer would effect in the way we understand understanding he explains thus: "The burden of my argument is that effective history still determines modern historical and scientific consciousness; and it does so beyond any possible human knowledge of this domination. Historically effected consciousness is so radically finite that our whole being, effected in the totality of our destiny, inevitably transcends its knowledge of itself" (xxxiv). Simply put, we are more than we know; our being exceeds our self-knowledge and the methodological self-control that is enabled by self-knowledge. This is to say that interpreters cannot ultimately decide what will happen to them, cannot regulate what insights will occur to them, cannot predict, control, or elude the effects of history on their understanding. "In fact, history does not belong to us; we belong to it," Gadamer contends. "Long before we understand ourselves through the process of self-examination, we understand ourselves in a self-evident way in the family, society, and state in which we live. The focus of subjectivity is a distorting mirror. The self-awareness of the individual is only a flickering in the closed circuits of historical life. That is why the prejudices of the individual, far more than his judgments, constitute the historical reality of his being" (276–77).

If one consequence of our belonging to history is that every interpretation is mediated by the prejudices of its time, if each interpretation is an effect of effective-history, then we are perilously close to the familiar paradox that all interpretation is misinterpretation. Yet the conclusion that all prejudiced understanding amounts to misunderstanding follows only if we assume all prejudices are false. Gadamer argues that this assumption is mistaken. A prejudice as such cannot be presumed either true or false, only methodologically illegitimate. That every interpretation is prejudiced means only that it betrays the marks of its birth, and such birthmarks have no bearing per se on truth and falsehood. We explain the errors of our predecessors as signs of the times; but if we are unwilling to concede that all interpretations that can be dated are ipso facto false and outdated—if indeed we affirm that there is something worth learning from past interpretations and from the past generally—we come to a revealing conclusion. Not only our predecessors' blindness but likewise their insight is owing to what happened to them. Some effects of history, some prejudices, were not just real but true. Our belonging to history is, to be sure, a cause of myopia; but Gadamer discovers that it is also a condition of insight into truth. Belonging to tradition, Gadamer writes, "is clearly not so much a limiting condition as one that makes understanding possible" (329). We understand not despite the impossibility of radical doubt but because of it, specifically because some of our prejudices are appropriate, productive, right.

But which ones? Which prejudices are conducive to true interpretation? We have seen that our being part of history implies that ultimately there is no theory of history that is not itself involved in historical practice. This statement already intimates that history is itself the ground of truth. To say now that interpretive theory cannot finally be divorced from interpretive practice suggests that theory alone cannot free itself or us from the false prejudices sedimented in that practice; it merely conceals them. For finite beings, there is no way to exorcise all prejudices, or to decide beforehand which prejudices are true and which false, or to escape the thrall of our false prejudices—except in the very process of interpreting. Not pure theory but "reflective practice"[9] is necessary to discriminate true from false prejudices, and it suffices. The true prejudice is the one borne out by interpretation itself. What distinguishes the true from the false interpretation is not a principle but a process, for to historical beings truth is disclosed in the historical process of interpreting. Insight, in brief, is not fundamentally the subject's doing, but an effect of history on those who belong to and participate in it. And for just that reason—because understanding involves not only what we want and do but also what happens to us beyond our wanting and doing—it is of interest to philosophy. For philosophical hermeneutics, interpreting, understanding, and applying are not ultimately the subject's actions. Hermeneutics is a passion.

9. By the term "reflective practice" I refer to what Gadamer calls *phronesis*, which, he says, was "first elaborated by Aristotle, [and] developed by the peripatetics as a critique of the theoretical ideal of life" (20; see also 307–24).

3

KANT AND THE

AESTHETICS OF

HISTORY

Given Gadamer's view that understanding is an effect of history, it is rather surprising that he begins *Truth and Method* not with history but with aesthetics and with Kant. Whereas Dilthey hoped to build a critique of historical reason on the foundation of Kant's first critique, Gadamer takes the third critique as his starting point. Grounding the study of history philosophically, he implies, requires a critique not of pure reason, or even of historical reason, but rather of historical judgment, analogous to the aesthetic judgment that is the basis of Kant's third critique. In part, then, *Truth and Method* offers what can be construed as an aesthetics of history.

Gadamer's initial paragraphs raise the essential issues. The historical sciences, he observes, seem neither to be based on induction, as are the natural sciences, nor even to progress in an inductive direction toward the discovery of increasingly comprehensive historical laws. This apparent failure is unproblematical if one accepts the characterization of the humanities as sciences still in their infancy, still hoping to discover (as research matures) the laws governing the sociohistorical world. But once one rejects the view that they are disappointingly soft versions of hard science, the real problem posed by the historical sciences emerges:

> Whatever "science" may mean here and even if all historical knowledge includes the application of experiential universals to the particular object of investigation, historical research does not endeavor to grasp the concrete phenomenon as an instance of a universal rule. The individual case does not serve only to confirm a law from which practical predictions can be made. Its ideal is rather to understand the phenomenon itself in its unique and historical concreteness. However much experiential universals are involved, the aim is not to confirm and extend these universalized experiences in order to attain knowledge of a law—e.g., how men, peoples and states evolve—but to understand how this man, this people, or this state is what it has become or, more generally, how it happened that it is so. [4–5]

History consists of particulars, Gadamer argues, and historical science produces knowledge of particulars as such. Usually, we say we understand a particular when we know the rubric or law under which to subsume it; we understand it as an embodiment of a rule or an example of a general category. But Gadamer's point is that, whatever may be true of understanding generally, historical understanding cannot be satisfactorily conceived in this way. General knowledge is certainly involved in understanding a historical event, as Gadamer admits; nevertheless, to know what constitutes a revolution in general is to know virtually nothing about the French Revolution in particular. Knowledge of how events happen in general does not supersede, obviate, or include knowledge of the historical particular. Were we fully cognizant of the laws governing individuals, peoples, and states, therefore, our knowledge of these laws would not suffice for understanding how this individual, this people, or this state is what it has come to be. To understand that requires in addition historical understanding, a way of knowing that can account for things not wholly governed by laws and consequently unique and unrepeatable. Because the predictive utility of laws depends on restricting their province to things of nature that remain always the same, a distinct non-nomothetic science is still indispensable for things that change and differ. Insofar as the French Revolution is essentially and not just accidentally different from the American Revolution and every other revolution, it is essentially and not just accidentally unpredictable. In other words, it is a historical event, for history is the event of the different, the appearance of the unique phenomenon, which no knowledge of law could have predicted.

The fact that Gadamer conceives of historical science as knowledge of "die konkrete Erscheinung" suggests one reason why Kantian aesthetics occupies such a crucial position in *Truth and Method*. To define historical knowledge in a positive rather than privative way, it is necessary to do more than contrast it to the knowledge acquired in, say, physics, for that contrast has traditionally led to derogating historical science as an inexact and therefore subordinate species of natural science. For a more appropriate model of historical understanding Gadamer turns to aesthetic judgment, since Kant had demonstrated the autonomy of aesthetic judgment vis-à-vis theoretical understanding and practical reason.

Beauty is, in many respects, a dubious choice of metaphors for history. "A thing of beauty is a joy forever," as Keats has indelibly impressed upon us, whereas history is the realm of the finite and temporary. Moreover, unlike taste, historical understanding ideally makes no value judgments; still less does it evaluate historical events according to the criterion of pleasure, disinterested or not. Nevertheless, overriding these immediate objections, aesthetics offers a promising way of thinking about historical understanding because both aesthetics and historiography address themselves to the particular, the concrete phenomenon. This concreteness, combined with the independence of aesthetic judgment in Kant's trichotomy of faculties, explains why Gadamer begins his consideration of history not with Hegel but with Kant.

In the *Critique of Pure Reason* Kant had drawn attention to the fact that judgment is an autonomous faculty, for conceptual understanding can never dispense with or govern judgment:

> If understanding in general is to be viewed as the faculty of rules, judgment will be the faculty of subsuming under rules; that is, of distinguishing whether something does or does not stand under a given rule. General logic contains, and can contain, no rules for judgment. . . . If it sought to give general instructions how we are to subsume under these rules, that is, to distinguish whether something does or does not come under them, that could only be by means of another rule. This in turn, for the very reason that it is a rule, again demands guidance from judgment. [177]

Here the nature of judgment in general is described in terms of subsumption. Understanding, the faculty that knows particulars as instances of rules, concepts, or other generals, cannot by itself determine which particulars are to be subsumed under which generals: it does not know which law applies in a given instance. That determination is the function of judgment. Because judgment guides the application of rules, it cannot be based on a rule, for such a rule of subsumption or application would itself require yet a higher rule to guide it, and so on in regress. The faculty of judgment, governed by no rules, is therefore autonomous from understanding, the faculty of rules.

"Intuitions," Kant writes in the *Critique of Judgment*, "are always required to establish the reality of our concepts. If the concepts are empirical, the intuitions are called *examples*" (196). By determining that a given concept applies to a certain thing, judgment supplies that concept with an intuited example, and so realizes the concept. The judgment subsuming "this flower" under the concept "rose" demonstrates that the concept "was not empty, i.e. devoid of any object" (188). So long as judgment is considered only as the "faculty of subsuming under rules," however, its value is limited to "realizing" concepts and showing that given rules do in fact apply to something actual. To subsume an example under a rule does not increase or improve our knowledge of the rule. To say "this flower is a rose" adds nothing to our concept of roses or even to our concept of flowers in general. Subsumptive judgments contribute nothing to concept formation.

Gadamer wants to claim cognitive value for historical science, of course, even though it is not rule-based. "Historical research," he insists, "does not endeavor to grasp the concrete phenomenon as an instance of a universal rule" (*Truth and Method*, 4). But since the understanding of history attempts to grasp concrete history as essentially irregular, it cannot be conceived as a process of subsumptive (or determinant) judgment. Historical understanding finds a closer analogue in the kind of judgment involved in aesthetic taste—which Kant calls reflective, as opposed to determinant, judgment: "Judgment in general is the faculty of thinking the particular as contained under the universal. If the universal (the rule, the principle, the law) be given, the judgment which subsumes the particular under it . . . is *determinant*. But if only the particular be given for which the universal has to be found, the judgment is merely *reflective*" (*Critique of Judgment*, 15). Reflective or aesthetic judgment fulfills the desideratum of historical study insofar as it gives priority to the particular over the universal, for what we want to understand in history is this particular revolution per se, and not just this revolution as an instance of revolutions in general.

When Kant goes on to say that "reflective judgment . . . is obliged to ascend from the particular in nature to the universal" (16), reflection seems to have collapsed into induction; and as Gadamer reminds us, "The experience of the socio-historical world cannot be raised to a science by the inductive procedure of the natural sciences" (*Truth and Method*, 6). By reflective judgment, however, Kant means something other than induction, as is clear from his assertion that "in respect of logical quantity, all judgments of taste are *singular* judgments" (*Critique of Judgment*, 49). The logically singular judgment proceeds neither in the deductive direction (all roses are beautiful; therefore this rose is beautiful) nor in the inductive direction (these roses are beautiful; therefore all roses are beautiful). Instead, the reflective judgment of taste lingers with the single, concrete particular in its unrepeatable uniqueness. And that uniqueness, in historical study, is just what is to be understood.

The universality toward which aesthetic reflection ascends is not the validity of a given judgment for all like objects, because taste judges an essentially unique object. If there were other objects like it, they could all be comprehended under a common rule or concept; but there are not. That is to say, aesthetic judgment is the archetype of judgment per se because each beautiful thing is unique and, therefore, the question of whether something is beautiful cannot be decided by rule. "To seek for a principle of taste which shall furnish, by means of definite concepts, a universal criterion of the beautiful is fruitless trouble," Kant explains, "because what is sought is impossible and self-contradictory" (68). Consequently, "there can be no rule according to which anyone is to be forced to recognize anything as beautiful. We cannot press [upon others] by the aid of any reasons or fundamental propositions our judgment that a coat, a house, or a flower is beautiful" (50). In aesthetics it does indeed seem that there are no compulsory reasons for accepting a given judgment of taste. This absence of rules, extrapolated to history, implies that the results of historical study cannot be demonstrated by appeal to reasons; and this inability to be demonstrated raises a serious problem, for what is historical knowledge if, like an aesthetic judgment, it cannot be proved?

Historical understanding modeled on aesthetics cannot be taught either, if that means teaching the rules of a procedure, since there is no regular method for judging or producing beauty. "Genius," Kant writes, "is a talent for art, not for science, in which clearly known rules must go beforehand and determine the procedure" (161). Again, "science [is] produced according to definite rules that can be learned and must be exactly followed" (156).

> Thus we can readily learn all that Newton has set forth in his immortal work on the *Principles of Natural Philosophy*, however great a head was required to discover it, but we cannot learn to write spirited poetry. . . . The reason is that Newton could make all his steps, from the first elements of geometry to his own great and profound discoveries, intuitively plain and definite as regards consequence, not only to himself but to everyone else. [151]

Taste and genius, in contrast, follow no rules established beforehand and leave behind no precepts that can be followed later. Unlike Newton's steps, those of the tasteful judge and the genius cannot be retraced or repeated. Consequently, just as aesthetic judgment cannot be proved by reasons, so also, unlike Newtonian science, it follows no method. But what does this lack of method imply for historical science on the model of aesthetics—that is, what are we to think of a science that cannot be taught because it has no method? Kant puts it simply enough: "There is no science of the beautiful" (147).

Still more problematically, the reason why "there can be no objective rule of taste which shall determine by means of concepts what is beautiful," according to Kant, is that in every judgment of taste "the feeling of the subject and not a concept of the object, is its determining ground" (68). The word "aesthetic" we recall, means "having to do with perception or feeling," and a judgment based on the feeling of pleasure is subjective. The universal toward which reflective judgment of the beautiful ascends is a subjective universal: namely, the satisfaction that the judging subject imputes to all other subjects.

For the purposes of validating historical knowledge, intersubjective consensus might be acceptable as a substitute for proof by
reasons, even if pleasure and feeling are in general irrelevant to it. But
for theory of history, the corollary Kant draws from the subjectivity
of taste is quite unacceptable. "Aesthetic judgment," he concludes,
"gives absolutely no cognition (not even a confused cognition) of the
object; this is supplied only by logical [that is, determinant, sub-
sumptive] judgment. On the contrary, [aesthetic judgment] simply
refers the representation by which an object is given, to the subject,
and brings to our notice no characteristic of the object" (64). The
logical judgment "this flower is a rose" adds nothing to our concept
of roses or flowers in general, though it certainly conveys information about this flower. A judgment of taste based on feeling, on the
other hand, tells us nothing whatever about the object but only
something about the subject's reaction to it. The judgment "this rose
is beautiful" is without significance as knowledge. A historical science modeled on aesthetic judgment appears, therefore, not merely
to yield undemonstrable, unteachable, immethodical, unscientific
knowledge but indeed to produce no knowledge at all.

At this point, it would seem proper for Gadamer to concede
that the analogy of historical understanding to the judgment of taste
can claim very limited heuristic value. Both share a focus on the
particular as such, but beyond that common denominator the analogy seems misleading at best and is probably a dead end. Gadamer
makes no such concession, however, for that would be to conceal the
real challenge that historical science presents to both Kant's epistemology and his aesthetics. If historical science, despite the fact that it
does not "endeavor to grasp the concrete phenomenon as an instance of a universal rule," nevertheless remains science because it
still yields knowledge, then not all real knowledge, not all truth,
resides in objects subsumed under concepts by subjects. If truth
cannot be equated exclusively with the certain knowledge discov-

ered by rule-governed procedure (that is, if truth cannot be limited to method), aesthetic judgment, conversely, cannot be confined to the feeling of beauty but is also a mode of knowing truth. This thesis—that taste has cognitive significance—indicates the distance Gadamer has placed between himself and Kant, although at no point does he simply abandon Kant's insights.

"Taste knows something," Gadamer asserts, "though admittedly in a way that cannot be separated from the concrete moment in which that object occurs and cannot be reduced to rules and concepts. Just this is obviously what gives the idea of taste its original breadth, that it constitutes a special way of knowing" (*Truth and Method*, 38). For now, we can call this way of knowing "learning by example" or "exemplary knowledge." In the *Critique of Pure Reason* Kant notes that "sharpening of the judgment is indeed the one great benefit of the examples," but he goes on to say, "Correctness and precision of intellectual insight, on the other hand, they more usually somewhat impair. For only very seldom do [examples] adequately fulfil the requirements of the rule (as *casus in terminis*). Besides, they often weaken that effort which is required of the understanding to comprehend properly the rules in their universality" (178). An apple falling from a tree may exemplify the law of gravity, but that law per se has nothing to do with apples and trees. For the purpose of understanding laws, such examples—all examples—are initially helpful but ultimately irrelevant, and, worse still, they are always potentially misleading.

In the *Critique of Judgment*, examples meet with similarly ambivalent treatment. On the one hand, Kant shows that examples of art are not just helpful but in fact indispensable: "Of all faculties and talents, taste, because its judgment is not determinable by concepts and precepts, is just that one which most needs examples of what has in the progress of culture received the longest approval" (125). Or, as Kant elaborates, "A Homer or a Wieland cannot show how his ideas, so rich in fancy and yet so full of thought, come together in his head, simply because he does not know and therefore cannot teach others. . . . Hence models of beautiful art are the only means of handing down these ideas to posterity. This cannot be done by mere descriptions, especially in the case of the arts of speech" (152). Since poems cannot be reduced to rule, and since description conveys no adequate idea of what they are like, we have no choice but to preserve and hand down what alone will give an idea of them: the works themselves. Therefore, Kant says, we rightly "recommend the works of the ancients as models and call their authors classical, thus forming among writers a kind of noble class who give laws to the people by their example" (124).

On the other hand, such examples, however indispensable, must not in fact be followed. Just as judgment cannot be rule-governed because it is the faculty of applying rules, and just as taste, though following no rules, makes its own judgment the rule for everyone else, so genius can obey no rules precisely insofar as genius itself "gives the rule to art" (150). This "new rule that could not have been inferred from any preceding principles or examples" (161), as we have seen, can be conveyed only by means of its exemplifications, the products of genius, the works themselves. But it is precisely when others take the works of genius as exemplary that problems arise.

> Genius is the exemplary originality of the natural gifts of a subject in the *free* employment of his cognitive faculties. In this way the product of a genius . . . is an example, not to be imitated (for then that which in it is genius and constitutes the spirit of the work would be lost), but to be followed by another genius, whom it awakens to a feeling of his own originality and whom it stirs so to exercise his art in freedom from the constraint of rules, that thereby a new rule is gained for art; and thus his talent shows itself to be exemplary. But because a genius is a favorite of nature and must be regarded by us as a rare phenomenon, his example produces for other good heads a school, i.e. a methodical system of teaching according to rules, so far as these

can be derived from the peculiarities of the products of his spirit. For such persons beautiful art is so far imitation, to which nature through the medium of a genius supplied the rule. [161–62]

The genius, then, is an example to two groups: to other geniuses and to mere "good heads." The first group poses a special difficulty: the genius is supposed to serve as an example to those who are geniuses insofar as they follow no examples. To avoid this contradiction, Kant suggests that to others of like talent the exemplariness of a genius consists in being not so much an example as a stimulus that awakens other geniuses from imitative slumber. Insofar as the works of genius offer anything exemplary at all, they exhibit the abstract quality of originality, that is, unexampledness. Because every work of genius (by definition) instances this same general quality, for the purpose of other geniuses only one work exemplifying it is absolutely necessary. Among the "good heads" with lesser gifts, however, exemplary authors replicate themselves more concretely—that is, they generate a school of imitators. From the fact that genuine taste and genius are untaught, immethodical, irregular, and unsystematic, necessarily follows the inferiority of those who teach or learn in the school, who adhere to "a methodical system of teaching [and producing] according to rules."

One wonders how even this inferiority is possible. How can rules be derived from that which is essentially not rule-governed? It must be possible, for genius is defined as giving the rule to art (to art of lesser quality, at least). Since the art of genius is based on no rule and cannot be conveyed by precept, it must be taught, if at all, by example alone. If genius prescribes a rule, therefore, the school must necessarily derive the rule from the example. As Kant avers, "The rule must be abstracted from the fact, i.e. from the product, on which others may try their own talent by using it as a model" (152). Thus, in Kant's exposition, the possibility of imitation, the possibility of abstracting the rule from the example, depends on the assumption that *the exemplary particular is essentially an embodied rule*, a universal, or simply an "ideal," defined as an individual being regarded as "adequate to an idea" (69). Even here in the discussion of genius, Kant conceives of the particular from the viewpoint of determinant judgment and understanding rather than from that of reflective or aesthetic judgment. This rationalistic conception of the exemplary particular (the classical model) leads Kant into a dilemma: insofar as the rule can be abstracted from the classic, the rule can thereafter replace the classic, which thus becomes dispensable; and insofar as the rule cannot be abstracted from the classic, the classic remains indispensable but cannot be in any concrete way exemplary.

Gadamer does not trace out the details of this dilemma, but he does draw the conclusion that Kant cannot: the "lesson" of aesthetics for our understanding of history is that the particular appearance is essentially unsubsumable. If one wants to understand the concrete, one cannot begin by conceiving it as an embodied rule; the particular phenomenon cannot be explained as an instance of a law. This conclusion is of considerable significance for understanding historical understanding,[1] for the fact that the rule does not exhaust the instance is precisely what justifies history's not attempting "to grasp the concrete phenomenon as an instance of a universal rule." This is no failure, immaturity, or inexactness on the part of historical science, for the nature of its object (namely, the historical event) dictates that it be studied in its own way. The concrete, historical phenomenon is not an instance of a general rule; and the

---

1. Compare Jacques Derrida: "Current scientific or logical discourse proceeds according to determinant judgments, the examples follow in order to determine or, in a didactic drawing, to illustrate. But in art and in life, any place where we must, according to Kant, proceed by means of reflective judgments and assume . . . an end whose concept is not given, *the example precedes*. The result is a singular historicity" ("The Parergon," 17). This historicity is Gadamer's focal interest.

real inexactness arises in treating it as if it were, that is, in modeling history on nomothetic science.

Modeled instead on aesthetics, historical science consists in exemplary knowledge. Gadamer is endeavoring to answer a very simple and therefore very difficult question, Why study history? There can be only one satisfactory answer: because the student learns something from history that can be learned nowhere else. Art history is the paradigm, because the work of art, most evidently, is precious and irreplaceable. No other work, and not even the precepts (if any) that can be drawn from it, can substitute for the work itself. From the work alone is knowledge to be had, if at all. What Gadamer really wants to argue from the example of art history is that every historical particular, every concrete phenomenon (and not just the work of art) is of potential cognitive significance: a historical particular offers the opportunity for increasing knowledge precisely insofar as it, like the beautiful, cannot be subsumed under fixed concepts already known. Thus he writes,

> It is only with respect to the exercise of pure theoretical and practical reason that one can speak of subsuming the individual under a given universal (Kant's determinant judgment). But in fact even here an aesthetic judgment is involved. Kant indirectly admits this inasmuch as he acknowledges the value of examples for sharpening the judgment. Admittedly he adds the qualification: "Correctness and precision of intellectual insight, on the other hand, they more usually somewhat impair. For only very seldom do they adequately fulfill the requirements of the rule (as casus in terminis)." But the other side of this qualification is obviously that the case which functions as an example is in fact something different from just a case of the rule. Hence to do real justice to it—even if merely in technical or practical judgment—always includes an aesthetic element. To that extent, the distinction between the determinant and the reflective judg-

ment, on which Kant bases his critique of judgment, is not absolute. [*Truth and Method*, 39]

In one respect or another, the concrete phenomenon always makes a bad example. It always exhibits a little more or a little less, a little something other than what is strictly necessary to exemplify the rule it is expected to illustrate. These respects in which the particular does not exactly square with the general will be dismissed as accidental and inessential so long as the example is regarded as essentially an embodied rule. But not dismissing them, and thus doing justice to the particular appearance as such, begins with a reversal of Kant's caveat: the same logic that shows that the concrete phenomenon does not exactly fit the abstract concept also shows that the abstract concept never exactly fits the phenomenon either. For knowledge of the particular as such, the concept is therefore not entirely adequate. To do real justice to the example requires more than recognition of the concept that it exemplifies and under which it can be subsumed. It requires aesthetic judgment as well: the recognition that the concrete is never a mere example.

Insofar as every example is in some respects a bad example, every act of cognitive subsumption that intends to be more than procrustean coercion must deliberate and judge whether and how well the particular actually fits the general, and vice versa. Such judgments are aesthetic. W. K. Wimsatt observes that whereas in physics apples are per se irrelevant to the law of gravity, in poetry "the apple and the tree are somehow made more than usually relevant [to an understanding of the law]" (*Verbal Icon*, 76); and whatever universal is exemplified by them is, since they are relevant, what he calls a concrete universal. So much is clear in Kant. But Gadamer, like Hegel, goes a step further. Taste is involved not just in aesthetic judgment but in every act of conceptual knowledge that tries to do real justice to the concrete, and thus Gadamer infers that "the distinction between the determinant and the reflective judgment . . . is not absolute" (*Truth and Method*, 38–39).

Doesn't this imply, however, that the distinction between the nomothetic and historical sciences is not absolute? Natural science is sometimes said to include an aesthetic element in that the simplicity or elegance of hypothesis is taken as evidence of its being right. But here we are concerned with something more substantial. All theories, Thomas Kuhn writes, "confront counterinstances at all times" (*Scientific Revolutions*, 80). In no experiment do the actual results coincide exactly with those predicted by the law; and, given this disparity, if Popper's falsificationism were taken literally, we would be left with no laws at all. In reality, of course, not every experiment falsifies a law or foments a scientific revolution. Still, each one might, and some do. What decides whether a revolution will or will not occur, Gadamer 'suggests, is an ad hoc, immethodical, fundamentally aesthetic judgment.

The fact that the distinction between logical and aesthetic judgment is not absolute does not imply, however, that the two are identical. In determinant judgment, when the part does not fit the whole, either the part is declared only accidentally discrepant or the whole is replaced in a revolution. In aesthetic judgment, on the other hand, the concrete phenomenon (the artwork) is taken to be irreplaceable, precious, and exemplary in itself, not just because it exemplifies a new rule but also because it does not exactly fit any rule. That lack of fit constitutes the indispensability of the artwork and the basis of its cognitive value. The work of art is never merely homogeneous with the whole, so that it dissolves into it and becomes invisible. Yet it must blend in. A judgment of taste must ensure that the work harmonizes with its whole setting, for the whole cannot simply be abandoned. Tasteful decoration must therefore do justice to the exemplary particular—to the uniqueness of the concrete but also to its fittingness with the general.

This is Gadamer's basic insight: genuine taste not only judges the concrete phenomenon by how well it illustrates the idea but also adjusts the idea in light of the concrete phenomenon. Aesthetic judgment consists in the infinite dialectic—that is, the circle—of part and whole, in which the whole undergoes a perpetual enlargement through the fecundity of the exemplary particular. This fecundity of the particular is not to be limited, as in Kant's framework, to the beautiful in art and nature. "Every judgment about something intended in its concrete individuality," Gadamer writes, "is—strictly speaking—a judgment about a special case. That means nothing less than that judging the case involves not merely applying the universal principle according to which it is judged, but co-determining, supplementing, and correcting that principle" (*Truth and Method*, 39). The subsumption of the unique, the integration of the autonomous, can occur only by expanding the whole. Understanding an artwork or historical event in its particularity is not merely a confirmation of a concept, rule, or law; it is equally an enlightenment, when, as if turning on a light, one can suddenly see more than before. Seeing in the light of the concrete involves more than understanding this work or that event; it involves expanding one's capacity for understanding, breaking through the rules and laws that have confined one's thought, enlarging the whole of what can be understood—in short, expanding one's horizon.

This is exemplary knowledge, the basis of the cognitive significance of taste. If examples do more than merely "establish the reality of our concepts" (merely show that the concepts are not vacuous), then genuine learning by examples, Gadamer suggests, is itself productive of knowlege and not simply illustrative of it. In this respect, he remains close to Kant and especially to Kant's exposition of aesthetical ideas: "If now we place under a concept a representation of the imagination belonging to its presentation, but which occasions in itself more thought than can ever be comprehended in a definite concept and which consequently aesthetically enlarges the concept itself in an unbounded fashion, the imagination is here creative" (*Critique of Judgment*, 158). Aesthetical ideas enable reason "to think more by their aid." This "more," in Kant's view, has no significance as knowledge, however, since it cannot be grasped in concepts and clarified by rules. But this view begs precisely the

question posed by the aesthetic: whether only conceptual knowledge, verified by methodical procedures, qualifies as knowledge and
truth. "Is it right," Gadamer asks, "to reserve the concept of truth
for conceptual knowledge? Must we not also acknowledge that the
work of art possesses truth?" (*Truth and Method*, 41–42). Making
this admission is the only way to take art seriously, but Kant does
not make it because he has already ceded truth exclusively to Newtonian mechanics. All the positive values he ascribes to art are
ultimately no more than compensation for denying its claim to truth.

To acknowledge that the work of art possesses truth, Gadamer
goes on to say, "places not only the phenomenon of art but also that
of history in a new light" (42). The fact that the artistic as well as
the historic is unique, unrepeatable, and essentially irregular had
seemed to prevent both from being ascribed cognitive significance.
Now, however, their truth-claim can be acknowledged because of
Gadamer's reinterpretation of the aesthetic. The understanding of
art provides an apt model for the understanding of history, he
shows, for the truth-value of both is that of the indispensable,
exemplary particular. More boldly, in light of the particular, the
concept of truth in general must be enlarged so that it is no longer
restricted to what can be grasped and made clear in concepts and
rules.[2]

In this new light everything looks different. If the judgment
of beauty has a claim to truth, and if beauty cannot be confined to
aesthetics, aesthesis, feeling, and subjectivity,[3] then the beautiful
comprehends everything that is "intended to be understood in its

2. Richard L. Velkley discusses this alteration in the idea of truth in "Gadamer
and Kant." Velkley does not discuss the relevance of Kant to the understanding
of history.

3. Gadamer speaks of the diminution of being that "the work of art undergoes
in being valued only as a work of aesthetic value" (40) in "On the Problematic
Character of Aesthetic Consciousness," an early version of insights later in-
cluded in *Truth and Method*.

concrete individuality." This includes historical events, as we have seen, but taste also "embraces the whole area of morality and manners" (38). How radical is Gadamer's extension of Kant can be illustrated by contrasting it with a more traditional reading by Jean-François Lyotard. Commenting on Dufrenne, Lyotard writes,

> It is not true that one can do an aesthetic politics. It is not true that the search for intensities or things of that type can ground politics, because there is the problem of injustice. It is not true, for example, that once one has gotten rid of the primacy of the understanding in its knowing function, there is only aesthetic judgment left to discriminate between the just and the unjust. Aesthetic judgment allows the discrimination of that which pleases from that which does not please. With justice, we have to do, of necessity, with the regulation of something else. [*Just Gaming*, 90]

For Gadamer, on the other hand, aesthetic judgment is called for wherever

> a whole is intended, but not given as a whole, that is, conceived in purposive concepts. . . . Judgment is necessary in order to make a correct evaluation of the concrete instance. We are familiar with this function of judgment especially from jurisprudence, where the supplementary function of "hermeneutics" consists in concretizing the law. . . . Our knowledge of law and morality too is always supplemented by the individual case, even productively determined by it. The judge not only applies the law in concreto, but contributes through his very judgment to developing the law. . . . Thus judgment, as the evaluation of the beautiful and sublime, is by no means productive only in the area of nature and art. . . . One cannot even say, with Kant, that the productivity of judgment is to be found "chiefly" in this area. Rather, the beautiful in nature and art is to be supplemented by the whole ocean of the beautiful spread throughout the moral reality of mankind. [*Truth and Method*, 38–39]

In this passage it is clear that Gadamer's ethical philosophy, like that of Lyotard, is heavily indebted to the *Nichomachean Ethics*.[4] But so also is his reading of Kant, for Gadamer identifies Kant's reflective judgment with what Aristotle calls phronesis. Like Lyotard, he would never affirm that legal, moral, or political judgments are or could be based on intensity of pleasure. Gadamer would go further, though, by claiming that aesthetic judgment is not based on it either. The difference, then, is that Lyotard limits taste to aesthetics, and aesthetics to pleasure. Such a circumscription, in Gadamer's view, itself constitutes complicity with the scientism of Kant, who reserves truth to nomothetic science and fails for that reason to take seriously the exemplary truth of art.

A similar inadequacy is to be found in Kant's position on the exemplary particularity of history, as well as in Hannah Arendt's exposition of that position. The pleasure that Kant posits as the criterion of aesthetic judgment is disinterested and detached from its object, so that the pleasure one experiences in art is that of someone who remains uninvolved and only watches—a beholder, a spectator. History too becomes spectacle, like a picture in a gallery, when conceived as something one can watch while remaining a bystander. In Kant's analysis of the German view of the French Revolution, for instance, it is the view rather than the events of the revolution itself that possesses exemplary validity. Not the "momentous deeds or misdeeds" of the participants, but instead the feeling of the detached spectators who view them, presages the moral improvement of the race. As Kant explains,

> We are concerned here only with the attitude of the onlookers as it reveals itself in public while the drama [*Spiel*: play, game] of great political changes is taking place: for they openly express universal yet disinterested sympathy for one set of protagonists against their adversaries, even at the risk that their

4. See especially book VI, where Aristotle develops the idea of practical wisdom (phronesis), differentiating it at once from techne and episteme.

> partiality could be of great disadvantage to themselves. . . . I
> maintain that this revolution has aroused in the hearts and
> desires of all spectators who are not caught up in it a sympathy
> which borders on enthusiasm. [*Political Writings*, 182–83]

Sympathy with those who are striving and suffering deserves praise,
no doubt; but spectative sympathy that refuses relief, enthusiasm in
a good cause that has no intention of participating in it, is merely
sentimental.

Yet the nature of historical understanding seems to preclude participation insofar as historiography concerns itself with the remote,
with events in distant lands and distant times. Moreover, because
history is unpredictable, and therefore cannot be understood in
advance, it would seem that it can be understood *only* ex post facto,
after the event is over. For more than accidental reasons, then,
historical understanding is detached from what it understands; and
it is just as impossible for historians to participate in the events they
want to understand as for spectators to mount the stage and join the
play. Disinterested pleasure, at most, can be expected.

Hannah Arendt celebrates the aesthetic distance of the spectator
in her lectures on Kant's political philosophy. Detachment defines all
sound judgment, according to Arendt, not only aesthetic judgment
but political and historical judgment as well. The detachment
of Kant's onlookers—who are "not themselves caught up in the
drama" and have not the "slightest intention of participating in it"—
displays the superiority of the contemplative over the active life.
"Only the spectator occupies a position that enables him to see the
whole," Arendt asserts; "the actor, because he is part of the play,
must enact his part—he is partial by definition. Hence withdrawal is
a condition sine qua non of all judgment. . . . Translating this into the
terms of the philosophers, one arrives at the supremacy of the
spectator's way of life, the *bios theoretikos* (from *theorein*, 'to look
at')" (*Lectures*, 55).

One doesn't expect help from moral philosophy in making moral decisions, and it is no objection to a political philosophy that it eulogizes the philosopher's way of life while remaining irrelevant for politicians. But the division of those who think from those who act is impossible when it comes to historical judgment. The closure of the bygone historical event, its autonomy over against the historian, seems to justify bringing in the aesthetic ideal of spectation insofar as aesthetic judgment involves a view of a whole by a viewer who is not part of it. Arendt goes on to say, however, that "the spectacle before the spectator—enacted, as it were, for his judgment—is history as a whole, and the true hero of this spectacle is mankind" (58). If all mankind is the protagonist in the drama of "history as a whole," one wonders, who is left to watch it? History as a whole, in distinction from some particular bygone event, has no spectators at all, only participants. It is not spectacle, because in the universal game every spectator is a player. In the universal drama every member of the audience is an actor, and in universal history every historian takes a part. Therefore, no theoretical and spectative as distinct from practical and participatory understanding of history exists.

Gadamer too emphasizes the role of spectator when he writes, "The spectator is an essential element in the kind of play that we call aesthetic" (*Truth and Method*, 128). But whereas for Arendt the spectator is defined by not taking part, for Gadamer what distinguishes specifically aesthetic play is that it is presented for spectators. In sports contests, spectators can become involved in all sorts of ways, encouraging the contestants or even interfering with them; nevertheless, the spectators' presence is finally accidental, for the game could go on quite as well, and perhaps better, without them. In this respect, plays are different from sports. Insofar as it is essential to a play that it be presented to an audience, the spectator always plays a decisive role in drama. "The play itself is the whole, comprising players and spectators" (109). The spectator is part of the play—an "essential part," as Gadamer says; and that is what is specific to aesthetic spectation, namely, that, as in universal history, everyone who spectates also takes part.

Count Yorck von Wartenburg figures significantly in *Being and Time* because, among other reasons, he discerned that history could not be understood merely as a picture or panorama. In his correspondence with Dilthey, cited by Heidegger, Yorck indicts the Neo-Kantians and the Historical School for their reduction of history to static spectacle and of historical study to spectation. "For Windelband," Yorck asserts, "history is a series of pictures, of individual patterns—an aesthetic demand. . . . But your conception of history [he writes to Dilthey] is that of a nexus of forces." And again: "Ranke is a great ocularist"; his "school was by no means a Historical one but an antiquarian one, construing things aesthetically." Heidegger himself writes, "If the historian 'throws' himself straightaway into the 'world-view' of an era, he has not thus proved as yet that he understands his object in an authentically historical way, and not just aesthetically." To assume another's world view is not necessarily to admit its force. In authentic historicality the history of what has-been-there is "disclosed in such a manner that in repetition the 'force' of the possible gets struck home into one's factical existence" (448–52 for all quotations). For both Yorck and Heidegger, aesthetic history consists in the view of history as spectacle rather than as force or a nexus of forces.

Gadamer concurs with this characterization of genuine history as force, and yet he perceives that "aesthetic" can become a term of abuse for inauthentic history only if one accepts an inadequate, Kantian conception of aesthetics. For Gadamer—or anyone who admits that the work of art is an origin of truth—detached spectation fails to account for the impact of art at all, and pleasure describes that impact in a far too anemic and patronizing way. Disinterested pleasure entirely misses the sense of the work of art as an experience: "In the experience of art we see a genuine experience induced by the work, which does not leave him who has it unchanged" (*Truth and Method*, 100). Rather than in the conscious acknowledgment of some pious prescription, some rule, the more primordial alteration effected by the experience of art occurs in the dawning of understanding itself, the moment of enlargement when one can see not this or that but simply further than before. Inasmuch as aesthetic experience involves the expanding and not just the applying of prior concepts, it is liberation into a wider ken.

The change wrought by aesthetic experience may be quite the opposite of pleasurable, and the very effect on the experiencer shows that the Kantian concepts of distanciation and disinterestedness are inadequate to describe it fully. For the other side of aesthetic distance, and what distinguishes it from objective distance, is aesthetic proximity or participation, the involvement that comes from getting drawn into a world, caught up in a course of events that carries us along. If art is taken seriously as a force or power for the reason that it makes an impact, it is like history when it is taken as something more than an object of disinterested inquiry, something more than the curios on display in museum cases. The historic event is precisely the one that cannot be encased or contained, for it generates consequences not just immediately but throughout an indefinitely long afterlife.

In principle, every historical particular, like every genuine artwork, possesses the capacity to challenge received universals, to enlarge the whole, and to expand the horizon of what can be understood. The historian who discloses the historic nature of a particular event by realizing its capacity to reveal a new world belongs to the continuing history of that event. It could even be said that the historian belongs to the event itself, for an event's consequences belong intrinsically to what that event is. A historic event is the history, par excellence, of its effects, including its effect on its historians. When it effects a broadening of their ken, most importantly, historians are part of the events of which they write the history, just as the spectators of a drama are an essential part of the artwork they view. Both art and history are modes of the unconcealment of truth: in the aesthetic Gadamer finds a symbol of effective-history.

4

METAPHOR AS

A METAPHOR OF

UNDERSTANDING

Just as Kant's aesthetics shows that the judgment of taste does not consist in subsuming artworks under the laws of beauty, so Gadamer's aesthetics of history, we have seen, implies that understanding history does not consist in subsuming historical events under historical laws. If not as subsumption, however, then how should we understand understanding? The new model that Gadamer offers, as already noted, is "the fusion of horizons." This phrase is not very clear, and in one respect at least it is troubling, for fusion seems to imply precisely the same suppression of particularity and difference as does subsumption. Yet such homogenization, I think, is not at all what the fusion of horizons means for Gadamer. He regards understanding, instead, as the kind of fusion that occurs in metaphor, a fusion that respects plurality while not relinquishing the claims of unity.

Although *Truth and Method* adopts prominent metaphors in crucial situations—notably the fusion of horizons itself—Gadamer has little to say about metaphor as such. Unlike Derrida, he has no apparent interest in the role of dead metaphor in philosophy, and unlike Ricoeur, he does not much concern himself with living metaphor in literature. In those few paragraphs of *Truth and Method* (428–32) where Gadamer does explicitly discuss metaphor, he gives it only scant mention—and then only in terms of metaphor-as-transference, conventional since Aristotle. As he is about to pass on to more focal topics, however, Gadamer remarks, "Transference from one sphere to another not only has a logical function; it corresponds to the fundamental metaphoricity of language" (431).

This last phrase—"the fundamental metaphoricity of language"—gives us pause because it makes such a grand claim in proportion to the attention here accorded it. Its importance becomes apparent, however, when we recall that *Truth and Method* climaxes in the conclusion that, in Gadamer's words, "Being that can be understood is language" (474). At the very least, this means that language is the condition of understanding anything whatever. All understanding occurs not through sympathy or even reconstruction but through the medium of language; and thus if language is fundamentally metaphorical, as Gadamer suggests, that metaphoricity must be reflected in understanding as well. One question *Truth and Method* raises, then, is what it would mean to say that understanding itself is essentially metaphorical.

In one form, this idea is not entirely unfamiliar. Paul Ricoeur writes of a dialectic between the understanding of metaphors and the understanding of texts. On the one hand, he says, "The understanding of metaphor is the key for . . . understanding larger texts," and on the other, "It is the understanding of the work as a whole which gives the key to metaphor" ("Metaphor," 100). I take Ricoeur to mean that metaphors are kinds of microtexts, as texts are kinds of macrometaphors. But this is not exactly to say that understanding is itself metaphorical, for Ricoeur's formulation still suggests that metaphor, whether micro- or macrotextual, remains the object or the occasion for understanding, not that it is a characteristic of understanding itself. Metaphor is not itself interpretation but rather the opportunity for it. As Ricoeur's early aphorism expresses it, "The symbol gives rise to thought,"[1] and yet insofar as it is a symbol, it is not yet thought. In *The Rule of Metaphor* Ricoeur similarly writes, "Metaphor is living by virtue of the fact that it introduces the spark of imagination into a 'thinking more' at the conceptual level. The struggle to 'think more,' guided by [metaphor], is the 'soul' of interpretation" (303). As Kant suggests of aesthetic ideas, so Ricoeur suggests of metaphor that it provides the impetus to think more, to interpret; but "interpretation," Ricoeur contends, "is the work of concepts"—of speculative, not metaphorical, discourse (302).

Between these two modes of discourse, in Ricoeur's view, there remains an "irreducible difference" (296). The semantic dynamism, the liveliness, of metaphor initiates and animates speculative discourse; nevertheless "speculative discourse has its necessity in itself," (296) whereas the metaphorical always asks to be translated into another discourse. Speculative expression aims toward the stable, the same, the univocal—while metaphorical discourse remains suspended in a generative play of similarity and difference that does not of itself terminate in a univocal concept. For just this reason, however, metaphor invites conceptual interpretation. It "includes a demand for elucidation to which we can respond only by approaching the semantic possibilities of this discourse with a different range of articulation, the range of speculative discourse" (295–96). Ricoeur's thesis, then, is not that metaphor and thought are merely antithetical, but rather that metaphor lures conceptual thought out of its complacent inertia by challenging it to think more. In this way begins the dialectical movement by which the distinction between metaphorical and speculative discourse is *aufgehoben*.

Without denying the suggestiveness of Ricoeur's analysis, we can discern that it is based on an incomplete notion of speculative discourse and, as we will see below, of metaphorical discourse as

---

1. This is the title of the final chapter of *The Symbolism of Evil*.

well. Metaphor, Ricoeur rightly argues, calls for interpretation, thought, conceptual elucidation. But, as Gadamer demonstrates, the same must be said of speculative discourse also. Like metaphor, speculation contains a principle of growth and plurisignificance. Gadamer, much like Ricoeur, allies speculative discourse with the Hegelian drive toward unity. "It is true," Gadamer admits, "that the claim of systematic unity appears even less redeemable today than it did in the age of Idealism. As a result an inner affinity for spellbinding multiplicity pulls upon us. . . . Nonetheless the exigence of reason for unity remains inexorable" (*Reason in the Age of Science*, 19).[2] Furthermore, "The tradition of metaphysics and especially its last great creation, Hegel's speculative dialectic, remains close to us. The task, the 'infinite relation' remains" (*Truth and Method*, xxxvi). Yet for Gadamer, unlike Ricoeur, the synthetic impulse toward unity does not exhaust the nature of speculative discourse.

By calling discourse speculative, we mean in part that it is not dogmatic: it does not content itself with the obvious or cling to received wisdom. The speculative person is restless, discontented with whatever is already given and eager to know more fully and think more deeply. It must be said of speculative as well as metaphorical thought that its reach exceeds its grasp, and for this reason the speculative statement too demands dialectical exposition. "My point," Gadamer writes, "is that the speculative statement is not a judgment restricted in the content of what it asserts, . . . a self-contained unit of meaning. . . . The speculative statement points to an entirety of truth, without being this entirety or stating it (*Hegel's Dialectic*, 96).[3] Since it does not state this entirety but yet indicates it, speculative thought contains its own impetus toward "thinking more" and need not wait for living metaphor to rouse it from

2. Fred Dallmayr discusses Gadamer in the context of comments on metaphor by Heidegger, Derrida, Ricoeur, and others in *Language and Politics*, 148–74.

3. Kathleen Wright is particularly helpful in explaining this in "Gadamer: The Speculative Structure of Language."

moribundity. Speculation, Gadamer insists, is of itself alive to possibility.

This is not to say that speculative and metaphorical discourse are identical, but only that they do not differ in respect to their invitation to think more. In neither case is meaning self-present; rather, it is virtual, always awaiting further development. Neither kind of discourse understands itself, as it were. Neither is self-interpreting, and precisely this shared lack of self-transparency accounts for the fact that both require understanding and interpretation. It is no doubt true, as Ricoeur contends, that metaphor demands interpretation; but conceptual language demands it as well. It may still be the case, then, as Ricoeur says, that interpretation feels the "opposite pull of two rival demands" (*Rule of Metaphor*, 303); yet the pull toward the determinacy of the one cannot be associated solely with speculation, while the pull toward the dynamism of the many is assigned solely to metaphor. In the speculative concept, the twin claims of the one and the many are already active.

The question thus arises whether the same is the case with metaphor. Gadamer too insists on the dynamism and fecundity that define the essential character of metaphor for Ricoeur. *Truth and Method* allies metaphor with the impulse to think more, specifically with "the freedom [of language] to form an infinite number of concepts and to penetrate what is meant ever more deeply" (428). Metaphor runs ahead of conceptual language because it need not wait for the work of abstraction, the determination of a shared identity, before being able to communicate the similarity of two different things. It is possible to say "man is a wolf" before we form the concept of "mammal" or "rapacious." Even before we have a generic term for the common denominator, we can express the connection of disparate things by metaphorically transferring the name of the one to the other. For Gadamer, as for Ricoeur, metaphorical expression is prior to, and is the occasion for, conceptual development. Yet the fact that concept formation relies on the fecundity and plurality of metaphor leads Gadamer, unlike Ricoeur, to the conclusion that there can be no dialectic between metaphorical and conceptual language because language is fundamentally metaphorical.

In this respect at least, Gadamer discerns the same universal metaphoricity of philosophical discourse that Derrida later elaborates in "White Mythology." "All the concepts which have played a part in the definition of metaphor," Derrida shows, "always have an origin and a force which are themselves 'metaphorical' " (54). Every discourse, even discourse on metaphor, is uttered within a metaphorically engendered conceptual network.[4] The metaphorical proliferation of concepts is therefore essentially uncontrollable—infinite, as Gadamer says. It runs up against no insuperable limit and finds no resting point in conceptual determination.

Viewed from this perspective, Derrida seems merely to radicalize and universalize the dynamism of metaphor that Ricoeur himself stresses. I have already argued against Ricoeur that the speculative concept itself contains an impulse toward dissemination and not just toward determinacy, but up to this point my discussion of metaphor has concerned his emphasis on metaphor's generative energy. It is important to consider as well whether metaphor also exhibits a contrasting, degenerative principle of entropy; and here again Derrida is of assistance.

Derrida's interest in worn-out, run-down, dead metaphors is not attributable simply to his focus on their role in philosophical discourse. Although his thesis is in part that metaphysics consists of effaced metaphors and that its work consists in that effacement itself, he does not conceive the work of metaphysics as an extrinsic violence, a murder of intrinsically vital, living metaphor. Rather, in his view metaphysics merely collaborates with an entropic principle already immanent in tropes themselves. Metaphor finds no fixed and

4. I borrow here from Ricoeur's summary in *Rule of Metaphor*, 287.

stable point in conceptual determination, even in the definition of metaphor itself; nonetheless, for Derrida the home away from home, this master metaphor, expresses the intrinsic tendency of metaphor not only toward movement but also toward rest. The figure of the borrowed home signifies, according to Derrida,

> metaphor itself; it is a metaphor for metaphor: expropriation, being-away-from-home, but still in a home, away from home but in someone's home, a place of self-recovery, self-recognition, self-mustering, self-resemblance: it is outside itself—it is itself. This is philosophical metaphor as a detour in (or in view of) the reappropriation, the second coming, the self-presence. ... The use of a metaphor to convey the "idea" of metaphor— this is what prohibits definition, but yet metaphorically assigns a stopping place, a limit, and fixed point: the metaphor-home. [55]

The metaphor of metaphor precludes arrival, as it were, and yet prescribes a destination. It implies difference, deviation, and excursion but also similarity, return, and reunion—so that a metaphor is at once essentially away from home and yet no less essentially at home there.

To Derrida's privileging of the home metaphor Ricoeur objects that this particular metaphor dominates philosophical discourse only to the extent that such discourse chooses to make it dominant. If this is the case, it is all the more significant that being at home is Gadamer's preferred metaphor for our situation in language. For Gadamer, language is the site of *Zugehörigkeit*, the locus of belonging where subject and object, thought and world, meet—or, more precisely, where they are already at home together prior to their having been split asunder by conscious reflection. "Language," he writes, "is an 'element' within which we live in a very different sense than reflection is. Language completely surrounds us like the voice of home which prior to our every thought of it breathes a familiarity from time out of mind" (*Hegel's Dialectic*, 97). And again, "As [language] is the one word or the unity of discourse, it is that wherein we ourselves are so completely at home that even our dwelling in the word is not at all conscious to us" (*Kleine Schriften*, 4:83; my translation). Since our dwelling in the word is not conscious, "Hegel's idea of knowledge, conceived as absolute self-transparency, has something fantastic about it if it is supposed to restore complete at-homeness in being. But could not a restoration of at-homeness come about in the sense that the process of making oneself at home in the world has never ceased to take place? . . . Is not language always the language of the homeland the process of becoming at home in the world?" (*Philosophical Hermeneutics*, 238–39).

Being at home, however, signifies only one aspect of metaphor: its implicit tendency toward rest, stability, and univocal meaning. Of itself metaphor tends to become literal and proper. Expressions such as the "arm" or "leg" of a chair are literal as well as metaphorical insofar as there is no more literal alternative to designate chair arms and legs. These expressions are the things' proper names; and in this propriety, an aspect of metaphor itself, consists its being at home. At the same time, however, metaphor is no less essentially improper since it always involves an element of alienation and difference, a divagation from the literal, or—in terms of the master metaphor— an exodus from the homeland. Movement, this second aspect of metaphor, is already manifest in the *Poetics*, where Aristotle identifies metaphor with *epiphora*, transposition or transference. If we define the literal as what stays at home, the metaphorical, in contrast, has been transferred and finds a new home away from home. The question, then, is why occupying a borrowed home is not just being "in someone's home," as Derrida says, but coming into one's very own.

When Gadamer addresses this question, he does so in the context not of metaphor but of *Bildung* and in particular of Hegel's conception of it. "Hegel," Gadamer writes, declares the world and language of antiquity to be especially suitable for [Bildung], since this world is remote and alien enough to effect the necessary separation of ourselves from ourselves, "but it contains at the same time all the exit points and threads of the return to oneself, for becoming acquainted with it and for finding oneself again, but oneself according to the truly universal essence of spirit."

In these words of Hegel, the Gymnasium director, we recognize the classicist's prejudice that it is particularly in the world of classical antiquity that the universal nature of the spirit can most easily be found. But the basic idea is correct. To recognize one's own in the alien, to become at home in it, is the basic movement of spirit, whose being consists only in returning to itself from what is other. [*Truth and Method*, 14]

Before considering this passage in detail, we need to note the unusual importance Gadamer ascribes to Bildung in *Truth and Method* as a whole. Bildung is, he contends, the mode of knowledge specific to the *Geisteswissenschaften*; and he argues that the human sciences of the nineteenth century, however unconsciously, owed their origin to this humanistic concept (18). Gadamer's thesis is that Bildung, not method, best explains the nature of hermeneutic understanding. What I propose to add to this insight is that Bildung also displays the structure of metaphor and that in a real sense, a metaphorical sense, we can say understanding is itself fundamentally metaphorical.

"To recognize one's own in the alien, to become at home in it," Gadamer writes, "is the basic movement of spirit, whose being consists only in returning to itself from what is other." In the structure of excursion and reunion defining Bildung we see at once the circular structure of hermeneutic understanding and also that of metaphor. Spirit consists in movement, and the first of its movements is the departure from its home into the strange and unfamiliar, the otherwise. If the move is complete, spirit finds a home, makes itself at home in this new place so that its new home is no longer alien. But at this point a reversal that is peculiar to the Bildung of spirit occurs, for the elsewhere that had once seemed so foreign proves to be not only the new home of spirit but its real home. We discover that what had seemed to be home when we left it was in fact simply a way station. The initial alienness of the other, the new home, was a mirage produced by self-alienation. The other is not merely opposed to spirit but is its own hitherto unrecognized possibility.

Metaphor, I suggest, is the linguistic correlate of the Bildung of spirit Gadamer describes. The literal suffers what appears to be an exile into the improper when it undergoes metaphorical transference, yet the result of this transference is ideally to assimilate and integrate the two things metaphorically joined so that the literal is released from its previous confines and expanded. Its extension is broadened; it now means more than it had meant before. The previous definition and determinacy of the literal are revealed as partial and incomplete by the success of the metaphoric transference. Through the assimilation of difference in metaphor, the literal finds in the other to which it is applied its own fuller propriety. What appeared as exile is in fact homecoming.

Spirit and metaphor, then, share the same mode of being: both exist not as a fixed essence but as Bildung, a movement by which something is alienated from itself and yet in that very process becomes itself more fully. Understood in this way, Bildung names the way of being that is specific to Dasein, for only Dasein "can say to itself," in Heidegger's words, " 'Become what you are' " (*Being and Time*, 186). Human being has no definable substance. It is "constantly more than it factually is" and therefore "is what it becomes" (185–86). Everything becomes and changes, it is true; still, Bildung does not mean merely linear alteration. What is peculiar to Bildung, the human way of being, is that Dasein does not simply become other when it alters, but rather it becomes itself. For Heidegger, understanding refers to the fact that Dasein never is but is always to be, and the process by which understanding develops itself (*bildet sich aus*) is interpretation (*Auslegung*). "In it [interpretation]," Heidegger writes, "the understanding appropriates understandingly that which is understood by it. In interpretation, understanding does not become something different. It becomes itself" (188). Anticipating Gadamer's fuller elaboration, Heidegger here establishes the equation of Bildung and understanding that underlies *Truth and Method*. As noted above, Gadamer conceives Bildung as the foundation of hermeneutics. The quality of understanding specific to the human sciences rests in the fact that interpretation alters the thing understood in such a way that its alienation is at the same time its realization. Alteration results in self-appropriation: by integrating something other into itself, or integrating itself into something other, understanding comes more fully into its own. It appropriates its own possibilities and becomes what it is.

Beyond the connection between Bildung and understanding, Heidegger addresses the relationship between understanding and metaphor that is of direct relevance to Gadamer. "For the theory of metaphor," Gadamer writes, "Kant's hint in paragraph 59 [of the *Critique of Judgment*] still seems to me the most profound: metaphor basically does not compare two contents but rather 'transfers reflection beyond the object of intuition to a completely different concept, to which perhaps an intuition can never directly correspond'" ("Anschauung und Anschaulichkeit," 13; my translation). According to this view, when direct intuition is impossible, understanding turns for help to metaphor. In the light of Heidegger's critique of Kant, furthermore, Kant's insight becomes even more suggestive, for *Being and Time* argues that intuition is not an alternative to understanding but is instead derivative from it. "By showing how all sight is grounded primarily in understanding," Heidegger writes, "we have deprived pure intuition of its priority" (187). The consequence of the derivative nature of intuition is that metaphor can no longer be conceived as a substitute acceptable only when intuitive knowledge is impossible. Metaphor becomes essential to understanding itself.

Once intuition loses its priority, it becomes clear that all understanding "has the structure of something as something" (189). Heidegger continues,

> That which is disclosed in understanding—that which is understood—is already accessible in such a way that its "as which" can be made to stand out explicitly. The "as" makes up the structure of the explicitness of something that is understood. It constitutes the interpretation. In dealing with what is environmentally ready-to-hand by interpreting it circumspectively, we "see" it *as* a table, a door, a carriage, or a bridge. [189]

Even though the as-structure of understanding that Heidegger here elaborates seems to have an obvious relevance to the thesis that understanding is metaphorical, his examples should give us pause. To take the thing I am now writing on *as* a table does not seem to be an instance of metaphorical understanding at all, for it is in very fact a table. Wittgenstein raises just this point: "I cannot try to see a conventional picture of a lion *as* a lion, any more than an F as that letter. (Though I may well try to see it as a gallows, for example)" (*Philosophical Investigations*, 206). It makes no sense "to say at the sight of a knife and fork 'Now I am seeing this as a knife and fork.' This expression would not be understood. . . . One doesn't '*take*' what one knows as the cutlery at a meal *for* cutlery" (195). For Wittgenstein, the question is confined exclusively to what it would make sense to *say*, what expression would be understood. Certainly he is right that we do not say "I see this as a table" but instead "this is a table"; and if in his analysis of the as-structure Heidegger is explicating any word at all, it is the word "is," not "as." The more important point, however, is that Heidegger is discussing not verbal reports of interpretive seeing but rather the "as" implicit in understanding prior to its verbalization. "Any mere pre-predicative seeing of the ready to hand," he asserts, "is, in itself, something which already understands and interprets" (189). If the interpretation is never made verbally explicit, and even if in an explicit interpretation the word "as" never appears, this absence "does not justify our denying that . . . there is any as-structure in it" (190). The hermeneutic "as" is prior to the apophantic "as" predicated in assertion: it is pre-predicative, pre-linguistic.

I began my discussion of Gadamer by deriving the metaphoricity of understanding from his twin theses that language is fundamentally metaphorical and that language makes understanding possible. Clearly, Gadamer's emphasis on language owes much to Heidegger, but in this respect Gadamer is indebted to the later Heidegger of *Unterwegs zur Sprache*—not *Sein und Zeit*. Unlike *Truth and Method*, *Being and Time* situates the as-structure of understanding prior to language. For just this reason, it clarifies the thesis being considered here: namely, that understanding is metaphorical. Beginning with Aristotle, metaphor has been assigned to the domain of rhetoric, and as a result, we have come to conceive it as a specific figure of speech, an identifiable form of language to be discriminated from other, nonmetaphorical forms. *Being and Time*, however, suggests that the as-structure of understanding operates in advance of language and therefore that the metaphoricity of understanding can be neither confirmed nor denied by the presence or absence or any particular figure of speech.

Furthermore, if all language is essentially metaphorical, as Gadamer contends, then this contention already calls into question the rhetorical conception of metaphor as a local and special kind of linguistic figuration. Thus the question of whether understanding is metaphorical cannot be decided by whether any metaphors are to be found in the interpretive expression of it. What I want to stress is that this conclusion holds even if, as in Gadamer's view, language is not something ancillary and posterior to understanding but is instead its condition, for asserting the metaphoricity of language does not imply that it consists of metaphors. (I suspect that this fact explains why Gadamer pays relatively little attention to metaphor as a rhetorical device.) If the metaphoricity of language makes understanding itself possible, the resultant interpretation will be metaphorical whether it contains any metaphors or not.

The notion of metaphoricity without metaphor can be clarified by turning to Gadamer's critique of aesthetic purism, for it is there that he relies most evidently on Heidegger's elucidation of understanding. "To do justice to art," Gadamer writes, "aesthetics must go beyond itself and surrender the 'purity' of the aesthetic" (*Truth and Method*, 92). Against Hamann, Gadamer argues that perception, even aesthetic perception, is not naturally or originally pure. It is rather "impure" in being always meaningful: rather than pure sounds, we hear a car in the street, a baby crying; rather than pure colors and shapes, we see a face, a knife, a wreath of blue smoke. Perception is instinct with meaning. Perception understands, and understanding involves the construal of something *as* something. "Every construal-as articulates what is there," Gadamer states, "in that it looks away from, looks at, sees together as" (81). Gadamer's analysis of the as-structure of perceptual understanding suggests that the hermeneutic circle of alienation and reunion operates at the heart of perception. Even with respect to aesthetic perception, Gadamer observes, "pure seeing and pure hearing are dogmatic abstractions that artificially reduce phenomena. Perception always includes meaning" (92).

The abandonment of aesthetic purism implies that art is indissolubly related to non-art. The classical term for this relationship is "mimesis," which Gadamer allies to interpretive understanding. Art "understands" (that is, imitates) non-art, and all understanding involves the construal of something as something. "As" means here what it always does: both "is" and "is not." Mimesis neither collapses art and non-art into identity nor segregates them into unrelatedness; it leaves them connected in the irreducible tension of similarity and difference characteristic of metaphor. Art understands non-art by representing it *as*, and this understanding is therefore metaphorical regardless of whether the artwork contains metaphors. In other words, it is the relation (between art and non-art), not one of its terms, that is metaphorical.

For Gadamer, all artworks involve representation-as, not merely those in which the representation is itself metaphorical—such as Reynolds's painting "Mrs. Siddons as the Tragic Muse."[5] Nelson Goodman shows why "representation-as" is universal and intrinsic to all picturing when he distinguishes two senses of this phrase. In the first sense, the "as" pertains to the object depicted; in the second, to the depiction of it. These two senses are not identical, and yet both are implied in any picture:

> With a picture as with any other label, there are always two questions: what it represents (or describes) and the sort of representation (or description) it is. The first question asks what objects, if any, it applies to as a label; and the second asks about what among certain labels apply to it. In representing, a picture at once picks out a class of objects and belongs to a certain class or classes of pictures. [*Languages of Art*, 31]

Goodman does not here address a third question that his analysis raises, With respect to portraiture, for example, what is the relation between labels predicated of the persons and those predicated of the portraits (themselves a kind of label)? Goodman observes that "everyday usage is careless about the distinction" (31), yet he fails to note that this very carelessness indicates the interchange that occurs between labels of objects and labels of labels. The epithet "picturesque" is transferred from the representation to the represented,

5. I have discussed this painting at length in "Mrs. Siddons, the Tragic Muse, and the Problem of *As*."

though landscapes are not pictures. Correlatively, the label "sad" is transferred from the object represented to the representation of it when we call a picture of a sad subject a sad picture, though pictures have no emotions.

I mention the example of the sad picture because Goodman employs it in his discussion of metaphor rather than that of representation-as. Defined as "an affair between a predicate with a past and an object that yields while protesting" (69), metaphor according to Goodman consists in a particular kind of transferred application, specifically, the transference of a label with an already established denotation to an object that resists that transference and yet accedes to it as well. If metaphor consists in transferred application, the sad picture is a specially significant example, because in this case the metaphor occurs not just when the term appropriate for a person is applied to a picture. Not only is the relation between representations metaphorical; so, too, is that between the representation and what it represents. If this same relation (between representation and represented) defines understanding, in the case of the sad picture at least we are again drawn to the conclusion that understanding is metaphorical.

Gadamer and Goodman's agreement goes beyond locating metaphor in transference. As noted at the outset, metaphor has been conceived as transference since Aristotle. Just as important, Goodman defines metaphor as application; and though Gadamer makes no mention of this connection, he identifies application as the fundamental problem of hermeneutic understanding. Goodman thus leads us to ask how application pertains to the metaphoricity of understanding.

As Goodman remarks, not every novel application of a label is metaphorical. Applying a familiar term to a thing we have never seen before is, however unprecedented, normally an act of subsumption rather than a use of metaphor. The routine application of categories lacks the conflict and tension that distinguishes metaphor, because in subsumption the category cannot be determined or in any way affected by that to which it is applied. In the Kantian view of understanding, discussed in the previous chapter, knowledge precedes application; and in applying—when it is thus conceived—no new concept can be formed. By contrast, Gadamer argues that genuine application (which does justice to the particularity of the particular) not only increases what one knows but additionally expands one's categories, what one *can* know. Genuine application therefore cannot be conceived as the ex post facto use of an understanding one already has, precisely because in applying one comes to understand. Application is an element of understanding itself.[6]

In order to explain how application alters and expands understanding, we need a dialectical conception of the relation between the particular and the general. Neither induction nor deduction explains how concepts are formed and understanding is furthered, because both are hierarchical and unidirectional: they proceed either from the "lower" particular to the "higher" general or vice versa, but not both. Understanding is furthered in application, however, only if neither the rule nor the instance to which it is applied is antecedent to the other. The act of conjunction that advances understanding can still be called application so long as we conceive of application as reciprocal rather than unilateral. Each term modifies and acts on the other so that they interact. Not unilateral action but only this interaction furthers understanding, for it establishes a common ground previously unthought of. The interaction that gives rise to understanding among persons of diverse times Gadamer calls *Überlieferung*; its correlate among persons of diverse language is *Übersetzung*. But most relevant to the present discussion is the fact that the intersection and interaction of two spheres of discourse within a single language Gadamer calls *Übertragung*: metaphor.

6. See *Truth and Method*, 312–24 and my essay, " 'London' and the Fundamental Problem of Hermeneutics."

Goodman considers metaphor a type of application; Gadamer considers it, at least implicitly, the archetype. Insofar as any event of understanding in the human sciences can be conceived as the reciprocal application, the interaction, of distinct spheres of discourse that discloses their common ground, all hermeneutic understanding is in that sense metaphorical.

Max Black, an early advocate of the interaction view of metaphor, presents it in this way: "A metaphorical statement has *two* distinct subjects—a 'principal' subject and a 'subsidiary' one. . . . The metaphor works by applying to the principal subject a system of 'associated implications' characteristic of the subsidiary subject. . . . The metaphor selects, emphasizes, suppresses, and organizes features of the principal subject by *implying* statements about it that normally apply to the subsidiary subject" ("Metaphor," 233). In the interactive view of metaphor (to employ Richards's more familiar terms), the vehicle is applied to the tenor, and their interaction consists most obviously in the fact that the first filters and modifies the second. If it consisted in no more than this, however, metaphor would be better characterized as unilateral action than as interaction. Every adjective modifies its noun; every predicate modifies its subject. What in Black's view makes a metaphor genuinely interactive, by contrast, is that the tenor modifies the vehicle as well. It is a simplification, he argues, "to speak as if the implication-system of the metaphorical expression remains unaltered by the metaphorical statement. . . . If to call a man a wolf is to put him in a special light, we must not forget that the metaphor makes the wolf seem more human than he otherwise would" (232). Because of this interaction, metaphor offers us a model of the reciprocal application that in *Truth and Method* constitutes the event of understanding.

Like metaphor, understanding involves two distinct subjects—for, as previously remarked, it construes something as something. In hermeneutics, the tenor is the historical event, work of art, or other representation to be understood; the vehicle is the medium of representation through which the work is understood. More specifically, the medium is comprised of the prejudices, the perspective, and the horizon already implicit in the interpreter's language. This horizon is necessarily distinct from the horizon embodied in the language of the work to be understood because without this difference no understanding can occur: to reproduce the words of a poem does not advance our understanding of it. Only as interpretation *in other words* can. Given the necessity for these other words, however, the poem is revealed only as far as the paraphrase permits. We project local prejudices, view the work from a particular perspective, and understand through a specific medium of representation that selects, emphasizes, suppresses, and organizes features of the text to be understood. Precisely this is also the function of the subsidiary subject, the vehicle, of metaphor. The relation between a text and its interpretation, I contend, is like that between tenor and vehicle.

If understanding is in this respect metaphorical, the charge that interpretation is intrinsically reductive must be viewed in a new light. Both the interpretation and the vehicle filter the meaning of the principal subject they represent, so that they can be said to reduce that meaning. Yet although metaphors are often enough accused of being ipso facto false or expendable, they are almost never thought of as reductive, as is paraphrase or interpretation generally. The foregrounding, backgrounding, and organizing effect of the metaphoric vehicle is precisely what enables a metaphor to provide an insight not otherwise achievable. In understanding, too, Gadamer suggests, the fact that the interpreter inhabits a situation and horizon distinct from that of the work (and filtering it) is not the obstacle of interpretive insight but its enabling condition (*Truth and Method*, 258–67).

As a vehicle transfers meaning to the tenor, the interpreter projects, applies, or transfers an already understood language-world onto the text. This projection enables insight in that only if the text speaks a language intelligible to the interpreter can understanding occur. Because the work must find a contact point with the contemporary world of the interpreter if it is to be understood, every interpretation, however fully appropriate to the work, will bear traces of the interpreter's present. So also "in the content of every dream," Freud remarks of Übertragung,

> some link with a recent daytime impression . . . is to be detected. We have not hitherto been able to explain the necessity for this addition to the mixture that constitutes a dream. . . . And it is only possible to do so if we bear firmly in mind the part played by the unconscious wish and then seek for information from the psychology of the neuroses. We learn from the latter that an unconscious idea is as such quite incapable of entering the preconscious and that it can only exercise any effect there by establishing a connection with an idea which already belongs to the preconscious, by transferring its intensity on to it and by getting itself "covered" by it. Here we have the fact of "transference." [*Interpretation of Dreams*, 601]

Like the vehicle of a metaphor or the language-world of an interpreter, the residues of daytime impressions "cover" the unconscious wish, censor it. Yet though its connection to the contemporary impression conceals the infantile wish, only because of this connection can the unconscious idea enter the preconscious and be revealed at all.

On the other hand, the transference Freud here describes occurs not from the contemporary to the infantile, but, quite the opposite, the unconscious wish transfers its intensity to the experience of the day. Not all daytime experiences get into dreams: only those that are selected, organized, and energized by unconscious wishes do so. Here we discern an effect very much like the back-pressure of the tenor on the vehicle that distinguishes Black's interaction view from unidirectional views of metaphor. In dreams, the unconscious filters and alters daytime impressions, while at the same time being covered by them.

This back-pressure of tenor on vehicle is crucial to *Truth and*

Method as well. Since Gadamer characterizes the transfer of the interpreter's familiar world onto the text as a projection of prejudice, it is all too evident that interpretive prejudices can, and in every case do, conceal the text. Even if the text to be understood, like an archaic wish, comes to expression only under cover of such concealment, we are still left with the suspicion that Gadamer's hermeneutics explains only how the present assimilates and subsumes the past, not how it reveals what has gone before. The application of a schema already understood, a prejudice already in place, to yet another instance does not further understanding at all. And worse, without reciprocal application, without transference from the past to the present as well as from the present to the past, Gadamer's hermeneutics will indeed seem only an explication of misunderstanding.

In *Truth and Method*, evidence of the interaction that occurs in understanding is not far to seek, however. In hermeneutic experience, Gadamer writes, "both things change—our knowledge and its object" (354). In interpreting an artwork we no doubt establish contact by transferring onto it an already familiar world; yet "the intimacy with which the work of art touches us is at the same time, in enigmatic fashion a shattering and a demolition of the familiar" (*Philosophical Hermeneutics*, 104). Thus we do not merely apply our prejudices to a text: "to understand a text always means to apply it to ourselves" (*Truth and Method*, 398). Such experiences are moments of Bildung in which interpreters are altered not so much by acquiring new pieces of information as by interpretive self-realization, coming into their own. The interpreter's horizon does not remain unaltered, as if it merely subsumed the unresisting text to which it is transferred. Instead, a fusion of horizons occurs, a reciprocal transference like that which characterizes interactive metaphor.

Does metaphor result, then, in fusion of tenor and vehicle? Max Black, in speaking to this point, cites I. A. Richards's warning that "talk about the identification or fusion that metaphor effects is nearly always misleading and pernicious" ("Metaphor," 229n). In much the same spirit, Fredric Jameson insists on preserving the consciousness of difference in understanding: "The Marxian conception of our relationship to the past requires a sense of our radical difference from earlier cultures which is not adequately allowed for in Gadamer's influential notion of . . . fusion of horizons" (*Political Unconscious*, 75, n. 56). What I would like to suggest in conclusion is that Gadamer's metaphorical conception of understanding does in fact allow for difference, while avoiding the Marxian trap of universalizing difference and thus making continuity unintelligible.

Metaphor consists in a nondifferentiation in which difference remains operative. Precisely this paradox is what Gadamer means by the fusion of horizons. On the one hand, Gadamer writes,

> Every encounter with tradition that takes place within historical consciousness involves the experience of a tension between the text and the present. The hermeneutic task consists in not covering up this tension by attempting a naive assimilation of the two but in consciously bringing it out. This is why it is part of the hermeneutic approach to project a historical horizon that is different from the horizon of the present. Historical consciousness is aware of its own otherness and hence foregrounds the horizon of the past from its own. [*Truth and Method*, 306]

Historians do not assume that the text's horizon is identical with their own, that the text is transparent and automatically intelligible. Quite the contrary, they posit a distinction between past and present. To understand the alien historical text therefore requires a corresponding self-alienation on the part of historians, an attempt to distance themselves from themselves. Yet, on the other hand, Gadamer adds, historical consciousness is

> itself, as we are trying to show, only something superimposed upon continuing tradition, and hence it immediately recom-

bines what it has foregrounded itself from in order to become
one with itself again in the unity of the historical horizon that it
thus acquires. [306]

The fusion of horizons thus described is a logically contradictory
movement of self-alienation and self-reunion. Understanding dif-
ferentiates intepreters from their objects, the horizon of the present
from that of the past, and yet in the same act joins them in such a
way that they are indivisibly one. Interpreter and object must be
simultaneously separated and joined if Gadamer is to avoid the
naiveté of both historicism (the belief that historians must escape
their own time in order to understand the alien past) and prehistori-
cism (the belief that there is no alien past but only pure, unbroken
continuity). How can interpreters understand something other than
themselves and their world, and still understand this other in a way
that contributes to and enlarges their understanding of themselves
and their world as well? How is it possible to think difference and
identity together? This is the question raised by Gadamer's explication of understanding. What I have attempted to show is that metaphor offers an answer. If we think of understanding as the establish-
ment of a metaphorical relation, it fuses two horizons in such a way
that they are both the same and different. Without mere contradiction, the hermeneutic "as" joins both "is" and "is not" ; and "in this
as," Gadamer writes, "lies the whole riddle" (*Kleine Schriften*, 2:22;
my translation).

5

A WORD IS

NOT A SIGN

The metaphorical relation between text and interpretation examined in the previous chapter does not pertain to special kinds of texts or interpretations alone. An interpretation as such is different from and yet also the same as what it interprets. Unless it is both, it is not an interpretation. If it is not (in some sense) the same as what it interprets, it is not an interpretation but a new text, unrelated to the first; and if it is not (in some sense) different, it is not an interpretation of the text but a copy of it. The concept of interpretation, then, comprehends two poles. On the one hand, it implies the fact that the text is continuous and self-identical over time, as well as the corollary fact that interpretations are necessarily *of* the text. This we might call the pole of correctness, since it explains why there can be wrong interpretations. On the other hand, interpretation also includes a pole of discontinuity and self-difference, in that the text can sustain interpretations that are not just duplicates of it but genuinely other. This we might call the pole of creativity, since it bespeaks the text's capacity to sanction an essentially limitless number of novel interpretations.

Both poles are definitive of interpretation. If the text had but one right interpretation and many wrong ones, or many right interpretations and no wrong one, there would not be a problem. The challenge lies, first of all, in retaining both the pole of correctness (it is not true that in interpretation anything goes) and that of creativity (it is not true that there is only one correct interpretation). Second, having affirmed both of these postulates, the problem is to integrate them—that is, to understand how there can be but one text and yet indefinitely many right interpretations. The temptation in thinking about interpretation is always to slide toward the absolutism of the one or the relativism of the many; but it is only by avoiding both facile solutions that we can glimpse the really interesting question, What kind of thing is a text that can invite many right interpretations which (being right) are therefore of the text but still different from it? This question is generalizable, for it pertains not just to text but to anything that can be understood. What mode of being does everything that is open to interpretation have, such that it produces otherness that nevertheless belongs to itself? What is being that can be understood?

Gadamer's well-known answer to this question is language, speech: "Sein, das verstanden werden kann, ist Sprache." This answer can be understood as more than a vague slogan, however, only by examining what Gadamer means by "Sprache" and how it differs from currently familiar conceptions of language. That difference is most succinctly expressed when he writes, "A word is not just a sign. In a sense that is hard to grasp, it is also something almost like a copy or image" (*Truth and Method*, 416). The task at hand in this chapter will be to describe the nature of whatever can be understood by describing language, as Gadamer conceives it. This includes both its critical and positive aspects—that is, we will need to consider both what language is not (just) and what it is (almost).

First, it is not just a sign. What this means is to some extent unclear, because, in his polemic against the semiotic conception of language, Gadamer evidences no acquaintance with Saussure, Peirce, or the figures who dominate current conceptions of semiotics. Because Gadamer's thought on semiotics is based on other figures—Plato, Kant, Humboldt, and Cassirer—his notion of the sign appears naive in some respects, while in others it seems strikingly fresh and incisive. Peirce was primarily a mathematical physicist, and his semiotics, however suggestive in certain directions, by no means concentrates on the question of language that is of primary concern here.[1] For Saussure, the case is just the opposite. Linguistics is Saussure's focus, and he considers it as "part of the general science of semiology," though "language, better than anything else, offers a basis for understanding the semiological problem" (*Course*, 16). A word is only one particular kind of sign, but it is also the archetypal kind. Since Gadamer denies the sufficiency of this semiotic conception of language, we can begin to specify the implications of his denial by comparing his conception of language to Saussure's.

Insofar as semiotics is simply the study of meaning, and "sign" refers generally to anything meaningful, there can be no objection to thinking of words as signs. But Saussure's thesis is neither so vapid nor so indubitable. "Signs that are wholly arbitrary," he writes, "realize better than the others the ideal of the semiotic process; that is why language . . . is the most characteristic" (68). By mentioning "others," Saussure concedes the existence of nonarbitrary, motivated signs; but because linguistic signs, in his view, are not simply arbitrary but are exemplary of semiology as such, arbitrariness comes to be not merely a peculiar quality of certain signs but a defining characteristic of all. "No one disputes the principle of the arbitrary nature of the sign" (68). "Sign" means "arbitrary sign."[2]

For this reason, a sign, in Saussure's usage, is not a symbol. "The

---

1. I have discussed Peirce in this connection elsewhere, and so need not rehearse that material here. See my "Hermeneutic Semiotics and Peirce's 'Ethics of Terminology.'"

2. Jonathan Culler makes this explicit in *Ferdinand de Saussure*, 112: "In the *sign proper* . . . the relation between signifier and signified is arbitrary and conventional—whereas the index and icon where the relation is causal or analogous, respectively, are by implication improper or degenerate signs."

word *symbol*," he writes, "has been used to designate the linguistic sign, or more specifically, what is here called the signifier. [The principle of arbitrariness] weighs against the use of this term. One characteristic of the symbol is that it is never wholly arbitrary; it is not empty, for there is the rudiment of a natural bond between the signifier and the signified. The symbol of justice, a pair of scales, could not be replaced by just any other symbol, such as a chariot" (68). "Sign," then, implies that (vis-à-vis the signified) the signifier is in principle replaceable and interchangeable; in the case of symbols, by contrast, the signifier is indispensable because uniquely appropriate. With these twin Saussurean theses, Gadamer is in complete accord. He denies only that words are just signs: though no one disputes the arbitrariness of the sign, Gadamer disputes the arbitrariness of the word, for he considers it to be in one important respect like a symbol.

Gadamer's philosophy of language assumes what Benveniste calls the speaker's point of view, in contrast to that of the linguist: "For the speaker there is a complete equivalence between language and reality. The sign overlies and commands reality; even better it *is* that reality. . . . As a matter of fact, the point of view of the speaker and of the linguist are so different in this regard that the assertion of the linguist as to the arbitrariness of designations does not refute the contrary feeling of the speaker" (*Problems in General Linguistics*, 46). To consider words as symbols expresses the irrefutable phenomenological fact that in actually speaking words are not arbitrary at all.

Initially, Gadamer discusses symbols in an aesthetic context: the romantic equation of the symbolic with art as such and the corresponding devaluation of allegory as unartistic. In the course of the discussion it appears that Gadamer's conception of symbol as the contrary of sign corresponds closely to that of Saussure. "The symbol," Gadamer says, "is not an arbitrarily chosen or created sign, but presupposes a metaphysical connection between visible and invisible" (*Truth and Method*, 73). Just as "allegory" means "other-saying,"—saying something more and other than what is apparent—so, as John Deely notes, "it's a contradiction for a sign to be a sign of itself: a sign is a sign only if it is a sign [of another]" (*Introducing Semiotic*, 61). A symbol, however, "is not related by its meaning to another meaning, but its own sensory existence has 'meaning'" (*Truth and Method*, 72). An allegory is heteroreferential; a symbol is self-referential, in that it is what it means. If "a poem should not mean but be," as MacLeish writes in "Ars Poetica," then a symbol that "is" its meaning typifies poetry or art as such—where "art" designates the inseparability of the how from the what, appearance from idea, form from content. More generally, the symbol symbolizes any indivisibility of signifier and signified. Symbols, in this sense, are not signs, insofar as the concept of sign implies the separability of signifier and signified guaranteed by the principle of arbitrariness.

"A symbol," Gadamer goes on to say, "is the coincidence of sensible appearance and suprasensible meaning" (78). In the symbol is implied the meaningfulness of form or appearance per se. In symbol, unlike allegory, appearance does not point to something other than itself; it means and is the very thing that appears. Since a sign is a sign only if it is a sign of another, the coincidence of being and meaning that defines the symbol is just what is denied by the sign. The symbol, Gadamer writes, is "not a subsequent coordination, as in the use of signs, but the union of two things that belong to each other. . . . The possibility of the instantaneous and total coincidence of the apparent with the infinite in a religious ceremony assumes that what fills the symbol with meaning is that the finite and infinite genuinely belong together" (78). In contrast to the symbolic, the semiotic as such implies that sensible appearance is one thing, that ideative meaning is quite another, and that the two are coordinated ex post facto: the finite and occasional act of meaning is fundamentally unrelated to the nonfinite and nonsituated thing meant. To call a word a sign implies that it consists in an intrinsically meaningless event of utterance connected to an intrinsically disembodied and unhistorical idea. It implies that sensible appearance, nature, history—things in general—are meaningless per se. Meaning is a function of mind.

After Kant (though not in Kant himself) art came to be considered neither supplemental to nor imitative of nature, but rather antithetical to it. "This switch to the point of view of art," Gadamer explains, "ontologically presupposes a mass of being thought of as formless or ruled by mechanical laws. The artistic mind of man, which mechanically constructs useful things, will ultimately understand all beauty in terms of the work of his own mind" (479). Coincident with this post-Kantian development in aesthetics is a significant reversal in semiotic terminology, for the mind's meaning- or form-giving function comes to be called its symbol-making capacity. In exercising this capacity, the mind gives meaning to what is of itself without form and void. Forming the formless and giving meaning to the meaningless, however, is what has been identified as the function of the sign, and it is of some significance that, in the neo-Kantian usage of Cassirer, for example, "symbolic form" is synonymous with "sign."[3]

Although in this respect Cassirer seems to equate terms that Saussure distinguishes, his *Language* (volume one of *The Philosophy of Symbolic Forms*) clearly belongs to the same Kantian tradition as Saussure's *Course*.[4] Cassirer describes his intent as "the description and characterization of the pure *form* of language" (*Language*, 71), and Saussure radicalizes the suppositions of such a project in his celebrated conclusion that "in language there are only differences *without positive terms*" (*Course*, 120)—or, in other words, "language is a form not a substance" (122). What distinguishes Cas-

---

3. Like Cassirer, Peirce and Benveniste use "symbol" in the sense of "arbitrary sign." I show below how such disparate usage is possible.

4. See Cassirer, "Structuralism in Modern Linguistics."

sirer's linguistic formalism from Saussure's, inter alia, is that he makes its idealist foundations explicit: the realm of language is— like myth, art, and all cultural realms—symbolic, which is to say that in it nothing is given but all is created by mind-forged symbols. "Here 'being' can be apprehended only in 'action,'" according to Cassirer, that is, as "an original act of the human spirit" (*Language*, 80). Instead of "the passive world of mere *impressions*, in which the spirit seems at first imprisoned, [culture represents] a world that is pure *expression* of the human spirit" (81). As beauty came to be conceived in terms of mind, so did being generally. If Cassirer had written "being that can be understood is language," he would have meant something like "being is an expression of the constitutive subject." Gadamer means by it very nearly the opposite.

Cassirer's subjectification of language is not limited to the cultural realm. For him the physical sciences exhibit the same "'primacy' of the function over the object" as do the human sciences (79). Indeed, Cassirer conceives of cultural symbol-systems as preforms of scientific symbolization: it is natural science that provides the paradigmatic model for all the activities of spirit, and science, not art, best exemplifies what Cassirer means by "symbol." Once "the naive *copy theory* [of knowledge] is discredited," he writes,

the fundamental concepts of each science . . . are regarded no longer as passive images of something given but as *symbols* created by the intellect itself. . . . Mathematicians and physicists were first to gain a clear awareness of this symbolic character of their basic implements. . . . The epistemology of the physical sciences, on which the work of Heinrich Hertz is based and the theory of "signs" as first fully developed by Helmholtz, was still couched in the language of the copy theory of knowlege—but the concept of the "image" had undergone an inner change. In place of the vague demand for a similarity of content between image and thing, . . . [the value of the image] lies not in the

reflection of a given existence, but in what it accomplishes as an
instrument of knowlege. . . . In this sense, Hertz came to look
upon the fundamental concepts of mechanics, particularly the
concepts of mass and force, as "fictions." [75–76]

No longer what Gadamer called "the coincidence of sensible appearance and suprasensible meaning," "symbol" has here has become the equivalent of "sign" and the contrary of appearance,
reflection, and especially image.[5] Cassirer's idealism must be considered one target of Gadamer's philosophy of language, for Gadamer
advocates the contrary thesis: that a word is not just a sign but
rather, in fact, almost something like an image.[6]

From Gadamer's point of view, Cassirer's conclusion that language consists of signs, not images, is the logical end of the path of
thought begun by Plato in the *Cratylus*:

> The legitimate question whether the word is nothing but a
> "pure sign" or instead something like a "copy " or an "image" is
> thoroughly discredited by the *Cratylus*. Since there the argu-
> ment that the word is a copy is driven ad absurdum, the only
> alternative seems to be that it is a sign. . . . Hence the critique of
> the correctness of names in the *Cratylus* is the first step toward
> modern instrumental theory of language and the ideal of a sign
> system of reason. . . . In all discussion of language ever since, the
> concept of the image (eikon) has been replaced by that of the
> sign (semeion or semainon). This is not just a terminological
> change; it expresses an epoch-making decision about thought
> concerning language. . . . Wedged in between image and sign,

5. For a succinct discussion of how Kant finally overthrew the resemblance
theory of cognition—and by implication the image theory of language—see
Sinha, *Language and Representation*, 7–13.

6. Gadamer raises questions about Cassirer's formalism in "The Nature of
Things and the Language of Things," in *Philosophical Hermeneutics*, 76.

the being of language could only be reduced to the level of pure sign. [*Truth and Method*, 413–18]

"The property of the sign," Derrida asserts, "is not to be an image" (*Of Grammatology*, 45). Eco and others assert likewise that an image is not a sign.[7] The question here has to do with the consequences and implications of this antithesis for philosophy of language. Cassirer, as noted, associates appearance and image with pre-Kantian realism and holds that the sign is "fictive," that is, it does not even pretend to correspond to that which it represents. Nevertheless, the sign is highly useful. This suggests the first implication of the antithesis of eikon and semeion. For Plato, as well as for Cassirer, a word-sign (which is no image) is an instrument. Whereas an image belongs to the thing it reflects, a sign as such does not, and thus its existence must be ascribed not to the thing but to the cognitive subject who creates and deploys it. Nonreferential, noncorrespondent, and fictional, the sign is not an image of the signified; but in the Kantian tradition it is still, for that very reason, an image of the epistemological subject, and specifically of the technological subject.[8] A sign is a tool. Conceived as a sign, a word is an instrument that the subject employs for its own ends—primarily, communicating ideas. One issue Gadamer raises, then, is simply this: is it sufficient to think of language just as a *means of communication*? Even if Gadamer adopts the metaphor of the word as image primarily as a tactic to critique linguistic instrumentalism, doesn't he

7. See Eco's critique of Peirce's notion of the "iconic" sign in *A Theory of Semiotics*, 191–217, esp. 202. See also Clark, *Principles of Semiotic*, 53.

8. Despite his critique of one aspect of linguistic instrumentalism (the notion that language is explicable as behavioral response to internal or external stimuli), Chomsky's Cartesian linguistics is nevertheless a prime example of instrumentalism in the sense relevant here, namely, language conceived as an instrument of subjectivity, of free thought and self-expression unaffected by the subject's immersion in its world. See Chomsky, *Cartesian Linguistics*, esp. chap. 3.

force himself into the universally discredited conception of language as resembling its object?

In place of the copy theory of knowledge (in which cognition is said to reflect a pre-given state of affairs) associated with Platonic metaphysics and empiricist epistemology, Kant substitutes a non-mimetic epistemology. Likewise he replaces mimetic aesthetics with the creativity of genius. Science too is nonmimetic, Cassirer explains, in that it devises "free 'fictions' in order to dominate the world of sensory experience and survey it as a world of law, but nothing in the sensory data themselves immediately corresponds to [these fictions], and yet although there is no such correspondence—and perhaps precisely *because* there is none—the conceptual world of physics is entirely self-contained. . . . The entire development of exact natural science shows that every step forward . . . has gone hand in hand with the increasing refinement of its *system of signs*" (*Language*, 85). Semiotic progress consists in refining away correspondence and developing an autonomous structure of signification. The "freedom" of science from its objects is corollary to the fact that its concepts are nonreferential and systemic: free concepts are precisely those that are, first, not copies or images but independent of what they conceptualize and therefore, second, useful in controlling it. The sign as such is not an appearance or image of what it represents, and it exists to dominate the sensible particular by reducing it to law and system, making it predictable and hence subject to will and desire. "The particular must not be left to stand alone," Cassirer suggests, "but must be made to take its place in a context, where it appears as part of a logical structure. . . . Cognition is always oriented toward this essential aim, the articulation of the particular into a universal law and order" (77). To say that a signifier is not an image of its signified is to say that it has no intrinsic meaning but only the "value" it receives from its place in the cognitive structure. Such systems of meaning are essentially ideal, disembodied networks of signification, formal entities whose existence and meaning is independent of their actualization (the event of their appearance). "What constitutes the true force of the sign," Cassirer rightly observes,

> is precisely this: that as the immediate, determinate contents recede, the general factors of form and relation become all the sharper. . . . Perhaps this tendency is most clearly manifested in the functioning of *scientific* systems of signs. The abstract chemical "formula," for example, which is used to designate a certain substance, contains nothing of what direct observation and sensory perception teach us about this substance; but, instead, it places the particular body in an extraordinarily rich and finely articulated complex of relations, of which perception as such knows nothing. [108–09]

Such formulas consist in what are called chemical "symbols" in the periodic table (for example, "Au" for gold). This usage of the word "symbol" explains why Cassirer can use it interchangeably with "sign," for "symbol" refers not only to religious symbols in which the symbol has a metaphysical connection to the symbolized but also to chemical, logical, and mathematical notations that are mere counters—instruments of convenience with no meaning except what derives from their position in the cognitive structure.

Mathematics has always been the prototype of this systematicity. For Plato, Gadamer shows, "being expressed, and thus being bound to language, is quite secondary to the system of relations within which logos articulates and interprets the thing. We see that it is *not word but number* that is the real paradigm of the noetic: number, whose name is obviously pure convention and whose 'exactitude' consists in the fact that every number is defined by its place in the series. . . . This is the real conclusion to which the *Cratylus* is drawn" (*Truth and Method*, 412). In our time, as before, the system of "differences without positive terms" is primarily exemplified by mathematics, and Saussure's semiotic conception of langue (lan-

guage as object of linguistics) is evidently conceived in accordance
with a mathematical model of science.[9] To think of language as a
sign-system assumes that words are essentially and at bottom numbers, albeit imperfect ones.

Gadamer is not alone in rejecting this view of language. In *Marxism and the Philosophy of Language*, V. N. Voloshinov's materialist
critique of structural semiotics censures Saussure's confusion of
word with number as betraying an unacceptable rationalism: "The
idea of the conventionality, the arbitrariness of language, is a typical
one for rationalism as a whole, and no less typical is the comparison
of language to the system of mathematical signs. What interests the
mathematically minded rationalists is not the relationship of the sign
to the actual reality it reflects nor to the individual who is its origina-
tor, but the *relationship of sign to sign within a closed system*" (58).
The prototypical signs are not words but numerical symbols.

Cassirer is fully aware of this fact: words are at best imperfect
representatives of signs, and for that reason linguistics cannot be the
master-pattern for semiology that Saussure envisioned. That place is
reserved for mathematics. In the process of working out the consequences of this fact, however, Cassirer implicitly calls into question
the very foundation of formalist, semiotic linguistics:

> The reciprocal bond between language and thought is . . .
> manifested in the logical and linguistic development of *numeri-
> cal concepts*. Only the formation of number as *verbal sign*
> opens the road to an understanding of its pure conceptual

9. This mathematization of language is evident as well in Hjelmslev, *Prolegomena to a Theory of Language*, where the author speaks of discovering "a
general and exhaustive calculus of the possible combinations" (9) that constitute
language. See also Chomsky, *Aspects of a Theory of Syntax*: "A real understanding of how a language can (in Humboldt's words) 'make infinite use of finite
means' has developed only within the last thiry years, in the course of studies in
the foundations of mathematics" (8).

nature. Thus the numerical signs created by language represent the indispensable prerequisite for the "numbers" of pure mathematics; and yet, between linguistic and purely intellectual symbols there remains an inevitable tension and an *opposition* that can never be fully reconciled. Though language prepares the way for these symbols, it cannot pursue this road to its end. The form of "relational" thought which makes possible the representation of pure numerical conceptions constitutes for language an ultimate goal, which it continuously approaches in its development but can never fully attain. For language cannot take the decisive step which mathematical thought demands of numerical concepts, namely their characteristic detachment and emancipation from the foundations of intuition and the intuitive representation of things. [Language] clings to the designation of concrete objects and concrete processes and cannot free itself from them even when it seeks mediately to express pure relations. [*Language*, 228]

The ideality of words, Cassirer argues, is prerequisite to the purer ideality of numbers; yet there is an "inevitable tension" and irreconcilable "opposition" between words and numbers, for in the progress of semiotic refinement words never achieve the perfect systematicity and abstraction from the concrete characteristic of numbers. This suggests that words are not merely imperfect numbers but are not, in essence, numbers at all. Words cannot be conceived just as signs (incipient numerical symbols) if, as Cassirer says, they are never ultimately divisible from "intuition"—which means from the appearance that the particular thing itself has. In sum, at the climax of Cassirer's argument, when the word is shown to fail as a mathematical sign, emerges the unintended conclusion that a word is something like an image, the particular's own appearance, and so also something like a symbol that is indivisible from what it symbolizes. A word that is not just a sign, that cannot finally escape history into the ideal, and that is inalienably bound to the concrete occasion and referent it expresses, has intrinsic meaning, not merely systemic value owing to its position in the linguistic structure.

But the tension between word and number emphasized by Cassirer is not simply extrinsic to language; rather, it is inherent in the word, for the word undeniably has an ideality of meaning insofar as words are not merely ostensive shifters (for example, the words "this" and "now," which take their meaning from the occasion) or behavioral responses to immediate environmental stimuli. And that ideality, whereby the meaning of the word is irreducible to the finite occasion and particular referent, exhibits the real similarity between words and the nonreferential signs typified by numbers. In other words, it is not accidental that "symbol" has such antithetical meanings, for however intimately the symbol and the symbolized belong together, they are not identical. It is possible to "desecrate" a flag insofar as disrespect to the symbol is disrespect to the country it symbolizes, but no one thinks the flag *is* the country. No one thinks that the word *is* the thing it means. There is always some discrepancy, some distinction, between symbol and symbolized, and thus something of a sign in the symbol. Even in the religious sphere, Gadamer writes,

> The symbol does not merely dissolve the tension between the world of ideas and the world of the senses: it points up a disproportion between form and essence, expression and content. In particular the religious function of the symbol lives from this tension. The possibility of the instantaneous and total coincidence of the apparent with the infinite in a religious ceremony assumes that what fills the symbol with meaning is that the finite and infinite [though by no means identical] genuinely belong together. Thus the religious form of the symbol corresponds exactly to the original nature of "symbolon," the dividing of what is one and reuniting it again. [*Truth and Method*, 78]

A symbol is what it means, but it is not merely self-referential, because it always points beyond what it is. Hence, like a sign, it is not identical to what it means. Like allegory, a symbol points away from itself, toward a beyond. But if the world of idea is not just beyond and if the historical world in which we live here and now—the world of appearance and of the concrete particular—is not mere formless void but genuinely belongs to the ideative world of meaning, then a word whose utterance is ostensively bound to that world is not just a sign of a meaning but has meaning itself. A symbol is always the same as and different from what it symbolizes. If Gadamer overemphasizes the sameness, coincidence, continuity, and unity of the word with what it words—that is, if he stresses the ways in which words are like images and symbols—he does so by way of corrective, for "nobody disputes the arbitrariness of the sign."

If there is always something of the symbol or image in the word, and the word and world are therefore indivisible, then it is necessary to reexamine the premises of the idealism on which the contrary, semiotic theses are based. As noted above, Cassirer bases his philosophy of language on the free symbol-making capacity of mind, where "free" means that the symbol does not derive from its object but nevertheless (and therefore) puts the object at the command of the subject. Since these two characteristics are correlative, to deny the arbitrariness of the word and assert its indivisibility from the world is to deny that the speaking subject can be understood as the maker of symbolic forms or the manager of its world. Asserting that there is something of the image in the word raises questions about how free from its concrete situation the sign-making mind actually is. To phrase this in terms of the aesthetic context from which Gadamer begins, once the symbol degenerates into sign, it can no longer be distinguished from allegory. Understood as sign, the symbol is independent of the symbolized, and in that respect allegorical. Likewise, when the symbol comes to be seen as a mind-forged expression of spirit, it becomes indistinguishable from allegory, for an allegorical representation by definition has no natural connection to the thing represented, and so has to be explained in the same way as the sign: not as an image of the thing meant but rather as an expression of human subjectivity.

What subjectivity is this? Though it is plausible to conceive the artistic symbol as the product of the solitary genius, such is clearly not the case for allegory, where the signifier is neither intrinsic to the signified nor created by any individual subject. Rather, it rests on "the anonymous intentionality—i.e., not achieved by anyone by name"—which Husserl associated with the life-world (246), which Heidegger called the "anonymous creation of meaning that forms the ground of all experience" (258), and which Gadamer identifies simply as custom. Allegorical representations have meaning only by reason of traditions of representation. Allegorical interpretation too preserves and extends traditions, specifically those so alien in certain respects that they have to be altered and so inalienable in others that they cannot be discarded. In both respects—as representation and interpretation—allegory is wholly traditionary. Thus, with the decline of the aesthetics of genius, the conception of the subject as maker of symbolic forms also becomes suspect. The increasing nondifferentiation of symbol and allegory and the consequent revaluation of allegory present a direct challenge to the freedom of the sign. That the sign is "fictive" indicates its freedom from the signified; that the sign is the product of genius indicates it is free of the traditions of signification. But just as the nondifferentiation of word from image and symbol (of presentation from what is presented) calls into question the freedom of word from world, so the nondifferentiation of symbol from allegory (of creative genius from re-creative tradition) calls into question the freedom of the word from the history of its use. Divisible from neither the concrete referent nor the concrete historical tradition of usage, the word is not, even at its most ideal, entirely free, not entirely a function of mind.

Wherever words come from, they are not products of genius. In a sense that will be considered below, the creativity of language is its normal condition, as everyone from Humboldt to Chomsky has insisted.[10] This is a creativity that belongs to language, however, not to any individual speaker, and thus it is no achievement of subjectivity. When Gadamer writes, "The sign acquires meaning as a sign only in relation to the subject who takes it as a sign" (413), he is most certainly *not* saying that the meaningfulness of language is to be explained by recourse to the speaking subject. He is talking about signs, not words, and affirming the position of Kant and Cassirer that the *sign* is an expression of the subject's freedom, though the word is not. On the other hand, when Saussure writes, "The distinguishing characteristic of the sign . . . is that is some way it always eludes the individual or social will" (*Course*, 17), he is talking about words and not the free constructs of subjectivity postulated by idealist epistemology. Gadamer and Saussure agree that, whatever may be true of signs, language is immune from deliberate change by its speakers.

Nothing is more human than language, and yet language is not human-made. Gadamer argues from this fact to its ground, namely, that language is coincident with, not subsequent to, the human, and hence is not be understood as a human creation, an expression of the speaking subject. "The word is not expressing the mind but the thing intended" (*Truth and Method*, 426). To say that the word is an image is to say that it is an appearance of what it reflects. The word is, as it were, world-made. Saussure, in contrast, associates the fact that language is not man-made or subject to human control with its arbitrariness—and we need to examine why he does so. "The term *arbitrary*," Saussure writes, "should not imply that the choice of the signifier is left entirely to the speaker (. . . the individual does not have the power to change a sign in any way once it has become established in the linguistic community); I mean that it is unmoti-

10. See Chomsky, *Language and Mind*, esp. 100, and Humboldt, *On Language*, esp. sec. 8.

vated, i.e. arbitrary in that it actually has no natural connection with the signified" (*Course*, 68–69). But the sign and the signifier are connected, of course, and the question is why the unnatural (but not human-made) bond should be called arbitrary. Saussure's second discussion of arbitrariness speaks to this question:

> The arbitrary nature of the sign is really what protects language from any attempt to modify it. Even if people were more conscious of language than they are, they would still not know how to discuss it. The reason is simply that any subject in order to be discussed must have a reasonable basis. . . . But language is a system of arbitrary signs and lacks the necessary basis, the solid ground for discussion. There is no reason for preferring *soeur* to *sister*, *Ochs* to *boeuf*, etc. . . . Because the sign is arbitrary, it follows no law other than that of tradition, and because it is based on tradition, it is arbitrary. [73–74]

Here "arbitrary" means traditional and hence unreasonable: there is no rationale for choosing one signifier over another, and thus, even if to use no signifier is impossible, to use any one in particular is groundless and arbitrary. Saussure asks why someone should say "soeur" instead of "sister." He knows, of course, that the reason is because others in the same verbal tradition do so, and the reason why "sister" means "a woman of the same parents as the speaker" is that a given tradition links them. But he will not accept this reason as reasonable. Quite the contrary, for Saussure tradition is no reason and is indeed unreason. Behind the arbitrariness thesis, then, is not just the mathematical rationalism that Voloshinov denigrates but also its Enlightenment corollary: the abstract dichotomy of the traditional and the reasonable.

This dichotomy Gadamer rejects:

> It seems to me . . . that there is no such unconditional antithesis between tradition and reason. . . . That which has been sanctioned by tradition and custom has an authority that is name-

less, and our finite historical being is marked by the fact that the authority of what has been handed down to us—and not just what is clearly grounded—always has power over our attitudes and behavior. . . . The real force of morals, for example, is based on tradition. They are freely taken over but by no means created by a free insight or grounded on reasons. This is precisely what we call tradition: the ground of their validity. [*Truth and Method*, 280–81]

Unless morals are to be considered unreasonable, tradition must, in some cases at least, count as good reason. The implication for language is clear. If tradition is likewise the ground of the connection between a word and its meaning, then that relation cannot ipso facto be called arbitrary.

What underwrites the arbitrariness of the signifier is an Enlightenment confidence, which Gadamer does not share, in the autonomy of consciousness from the concrete historical world. This confidence is most apparent in Saussure's segregation of the object of linguistics from the speaking of language: his distinction between langue and parole. In a passage preparing for this divorce of language from event, meaning from history, Saussure writes,

Consider, for example, the production of sounds necessary for speaking. The vocal organs are as external to language as are the electrical devices used in transmitting the Morse code to the code itself; and phonation, i.e., the execution of sound-images, in no way affects the system itself. Language is comparable to a symphony in that what the symphony actually is stands completely apart from how it is performed; the mistakes that musicians make in playing the symphony do not compromise this fact. [*Course*, 18]

Saussure here appeals not only to Kantian philosophy of science but also to a formalist aesthetics. Corollary to the autonomy of langue from parole is the autonomy of the artwork from its presentation, and both are derivative of the autonomy of consciousness from its world. Just as for Wimsatt and Beardsley in "The Affective Fallacy," the poem as such is not to be confused with readers' reactions to it (Wimsatt, *Verbal Icon*, 20–39), so for Saussure what the symphony actually is, is independent of its performance, its interpretation. As Saussure associates tradition with unreason, so he associates performance with contingency and error.

Though Saussure is certainly right that the symphony as such is unaltered by the mistakes of musicians, it is surely odd to suggest that sound is wholly accidental to what a symphony actually is. Saussure affirms the self-identity of the symphony and the principle of correctness based on it, but in rightly insisting that the possibility of mistake is intrinsic to interpretation, he veers to the opposite extreme of inferring that all performance is mistaken, all interpretation misinterpretation—which is to say that interpretation is impossible.

The differentiation of the symphony from the interpretations of it Gadamer calls "aesthetic" differentiation, because in distinguishing between the artwork and its performance, it abstracts the aesthetic as such from the nonaesthetic. Without repeating Gadamer's argument against such differentiation in detail, it is important to reiterate that it depends on a salient fact: music that does not resound is not music. The music played is the music itself. Since a symphony exists most concretely in actual performance rather than in the score or in the head of the composer, it is inherently indivisible from its performance, and there must, therefore, be some performance that is a presentation of the symphony itself, its own image and appearance. "The work of art," Gadamer asserts, "experiences a continued determination of its meaning from the 'occasion' of its coming-to-presentation. . . . Every performance is an event, but not one in any way separate from the work—the work itself is what 'takes place' (ereignet) in the event (Ereignis) of performance" (*Truth and Method*, 147). The performance is the appearance of the work, the work's own appearance, the event of its self-presentation, which (being its own image) cannot be divided from it. The reason why the performance cannot be divided from the symphony is that the performance is the very symphony itself, and interpretation therefore cannot be conceived as something the interpreting subject does to an object. Only mistaken interpretations can be explained by appeal to the musicians. The performance that is the appearance of the symphony itself, however, is its own *self*-interpretation. "Obviously it is not peculiar to the work of art that it has its being in its presentation" (476), Gadamer goes on to say. Everything that can be understood is self-presentation. We will need to return to this below.

The linguistic analogue of aesthetic differentiation—namely, the differentiation of langue and parole—distinguishes language as such from all that is incidental to it. Implied in abstracting down to the word as word (or art as art) is that the concrete event of appearance is irrelevant, meaningless per se, and intrinsically unrelated to the thing itself. The word as such is just a sign, and a sign receives its signification from the system, not from the signified or (most relevant here) from the event of signing. If, on the other hand, the word is not just a sign, as Gadamer would have us believe, then its being almost an image suggests that langue is inalienable from parole. The world is as indivisible from its coming to language, and the meaning of a word is as indivisible from its utterance, as is a symphony from its performance and an image from the thing it reflects.

Even those who are willing to admit that in the performing arts the art cannot be abstracted from the performance may not, however, be convinced that the same is true of the other arts. But such an extrapolation is especially necessary for Gadamer's argument insofar as vision and the visual arts form the metaphorical context of his conception of the word as image. A symphony, perhaps, cannot be absolutely dichotomized from its performances, but what is the equivalent of performance in the case of a picture? We might say that paintings are "performed" when they are hung, situated in a context, placed in a new world, as a repertory play is recontextualized when it is performed before a modern audience. Alternatively, we might say a picture is "performed" by being imitated; but in fact imitations of a painting, however perfect, are hardly to be confused with the picture itself. To present a picture, Gadamer acknowledges, cannot mean to copy it (138). The same is true of the performance of a drama, which is not a copy either. Moreover, just as to present a painting does not mean to copy it, so to be presented in a painting does not mean to be copied, especially if the painting is a work of art. A picture neither copies nor is copyable. Yet Plato must be reckoned with, and Gadamer does so in his discussion of the relation of copy, image, and picture. In reviewing this discussion, we need to keep in mind that Gadamer is considering the nature not only of picturing but of language as well.[11]

A copy loses itself in accomplishing its end, namely, to point to something not itself. The function of copying is fulfilled when the copy effaces itself in pure reference to what it copies. In this respect the ideal copy is a mirror image, which is called "virtual" because it has no real existence and is thus perfectly "effaced"; the mirror has no image, for the image is of the thing itself that it reflects. A copy, though, is not an image because it has a real existence independent of what it copies. A picture is like a copy in this respect, for it too has a real existence autonomous from what is pictured. Yet the picture differs from the copy in refusing to efface itself and instead affirming its own being; it cannot be reduced to what it presents.

A picture has something of both copy and mirror image. It need not look the same as what is pictured, yet as the German language insists, a picture (*Bild*) is an image (*Bild*), an appearance of the very thing it pictures. We begin to see that in his discussion of picturing

11. One of the few to consider images as signs, Virgil C. Aldrich, covers some of the same ground as Gadamer (without mentioning him, and to other ends) in "Mirrors, Pictures, Words, Perceptions."

Gadamer is trying to resolve the aporia of mimesis—either an imitation is identical to what it imitates and hence superfluous, or it is
unrelated to what it imitates and hence a lie. But at the same time he
is addressing the aporia of interpretation, which is a variant of the
former. A picture is an interpretation of what it pictures. In being no
copy, a picture exemplifies the principle of interpretive creativity,
namely, that a genuine interpretation is never identical to what it
interprets. Yet in being an image, a picture exemplifies the principle
of correctness as well, in that it cannot be absolutely differentiated
from the thing it pictures insofar as it is a picture *of* that thing and so
belongs to it. Now, what must be the being of what is picturable,
such that it presents itself in interpretations that are different from it
and have their own being, but are nevertheless *of itself*?

For Gadamer, the picture-image is a model of being that can be
understood—that is, of language. "The essence of the picture," he
writes, "is situated, as it were, halfway between two extremes: these
extremes of representation are *pure indication* (Verweisung), which
is the essence of the sign, and *pure substitution* (Vertreten), which is
the essence of the symbol. There is something of both in a picture"
(152). It is not just a sign and not quite a symbol. A picture is not a
sign in that we linger over it and do not merely look through and
away from it toward something else; one can understand what a
picture pictures only by looking at the picture itself. Moreover,
whereas what a sign refers to is not present, what a picture represents presents itself in the picture. (This is merely another way of
saying that it is a picture *of the thing*.) The picture is the self-
presentation of what it depicts: the appearance of the thing itself. It
can be presented in other pictures as well, to be sure, but that does
not prove all pictures are arbitrary; it proves that what is pictured
can present itself in various ways. Furthermore, not only is a picture
not a sign; a picture is not a symbol either. Like the symbol, a picture
represents what is present (not what is absent, like the sign): one
does not look through the picture at something else. Yet a picture is

unlike a symbol in that through being pictured the thing depicted is not merely affirmed as present; rather, it presents itself otherwise, different from itself, as depicted in the autonomous being of the picture. In Neoplatonic language, the picture is an emanation of what it depicts; the autonomous being of the picture is an emanation of the other from the same. In Gadamer's language, the picture is an event of being, for in presenting itself (otherwise) in the picture the thing is (itself) more fully.

What about the thing in itself and apart from any and all pictures of it? Gadamer responds in the spirit of Hegel: "The quality of being-in-itself that distinguishes the thing-in-itself from its appearance is in-itself only for us" (343). "A person who opposes 'being-in-itself' to these 'aspects' [that is, appearances] must think either theologically—in which case 'being-in-itself' is not for him but only for God—or he will think like Lucifer, like one who wants to prove his own divinity by the fact that the whole world has to obey him" (448). To think like neither, however, is to refuse to dichotomize symphony from performance, the interpreted from its interpretation, the pictured from the picture, being in itself from its appearance.

This refusal has several implications: first, language cannot be dichotomized from its performance, its utterance. The langue/parole distinction falsifies what language is, for a word is a word uttered, a word in dialogue. Further, the langue/parole distinction posits a word in itself, just as the signifier/signified distinction posits a signified in itself. When Gadamer affirms that the word is almost like an image, however, he means (in Saussure's terms) that signified cannot be divided from signifier and that however undeniably "the linguistic unit is a double entity," as Saussure insists (*Course*, 65), it is no less undeniably a unitary entity. It is split yet integral—and to the extent that the word is indecomposably one, there is neither signifier nor signified. That is a Platonic distinction, and as Occam would say, a distinction without a difference. The fact of arbitrariness, Saussure writes, "is proved by differences among languages and by the very existence of languages" (68). That one and the same signified can be represented by an indefinitely large number of signifiers, as in the case of translation, demonstrates the arbitrariness of the signifier. But as Derrida has shown, Saussure's proof assumes that the signified is knowable apart from any signifier whatever; the notion of arbitrariness so defined postulates a transcendental signified that, in Derrida's words, would escape "the play of signifying references that constitute language" (*Of Grammatology*, 7). Just as Gadamer posits no word apart from utterance, he, unlike Saussure but like Derrida, postulates no being in itself that would be independent of its appearance in language. The word is inalienable from its utterance, and exactly the same is true of what is said: the thing meant is not "in itself" such that the word would have to advene to it from without. The thing itself appears in language.

This should be underscored: no being in itself implies no being independent of appearance. In terms of pictures, we can say being that is picturable appears, presents itself, images itself. Language is the appearance of being, its own image, its own self-reflection. In terms of interpretation, we can say that being that images itself interprets itself in language. Being that can be understood, interpretable being, is not "in itself" such that the interpretation (the verbal appearance of the understanding) is superadded. Being that can be understood appears, presents itself, performs itself, pictures itself, interprets itself in words: being that can be understood therefore *is* (inalienable from) language. Even though translation—Saussure's exemplar of the interchangability of the signifier—has been taken as the model of all hermeneutics, Gadamer speaks of "the agony of translation," not the ease with which Saussure supposes any signifier can be replaced with any other. That agony stems from the fact that "the original words seem to be inseparable from the things they refer to" (*Truth and Method*, 402). It is this intimate unity of language and thought—and ultimately, language and being—that Gadamer affirms by asserting that the word is something like an image that belongs to what it reflects.

He does not mean that there is any similarity or resemblance between word and world. Resemblance is one kind of belonging-together, and the fact that it clearly is not the kind exemplified in the relation of language and world does not constitute a reason for denying that they belong together in some way. "Language and thinking about things are so bound together," Gadamer says, "that it is an abstraction to conceive of the system of truths as a pregiven system of possibilities of being for which the signifying subject selects corresponding signs" (417). The similarity theory is wrong not because there is no similarity between signifier and signified but because there is no difference either, since there is no opportunity for comparison at all. Everyone agrees that the best model for under-standing language is not that of nomenclature, the assigning of signifiers ex post facto to things given beforehand. Something like that is assumed, nevertheless, not only by the similarity theory but also by the arbitrariness principle that is its opposite: as if one could somehow hold up a wordless world in one hand and a worldless word in the other, and determine that the two do or do not match. "Experience [of the world] is not wordless to begin with," Gadamer argues. "Rather, experience of itself seeks and finds words that express it. We seek the right word—i.e., the word that really belongs to the thing—so that in it the thing comes into language" (417). The human world is always already a language world, and for exactly that reason the human word is always and in every case worlded.[12] If comparing world and word is therefore impossible, Gadamer infers, "we may speak of an *absolute perfection of the word*, in-asmuch as there is no perceptible relationship—i.e., no gap—be-

12. Joseph Margolis has recently come to the same conclusion in "The Human Voice of Semiotics": "There is no difference between languaged world and worlded language."

tween its appearance to the senses and its meaning" (410). "Not only is the world world only insofar as it comes into language," in Gadamer's view, "but language, too, has its real being only in the fact that the world is presented in it" (443). This is one reason why all attempts at a formal description of language must fail: if every human word is always and in every case indivisible from the world, language is not a form.

That does not mean it is a substance, of course. The point is that language is neither a substance nor a form. In fact it is characteristic of linguistic formalisms to be hoist on their own petard: they substantialize form itself, for they hypostatize language as an entity (a structure) that can be studied independent of its saying anything at all.[13] The question, then, is, What kind of thing is language if it is neither form nor substance? Gadamer's response (and this is a second reason for the failure of formal linguistics) is that language is a process or event. If that is the case, we need to interpret the spatial metaphors of image and picture temporally, and thus reintroduce history into the description of being that can be understood.

A word is not an existent thing. The Saussurean notion of a system of differences takes cognizance of that. But in challenging linguistic formalism, Gadamer insists that "a word is a process" (434), an ongoing history. In this respect he aligns himself with Humboldt. Despite Humboldt's tendency toward a subjective formalism,[14] Gadamer fully concurs when Humboldt speaks of "the way in which the distant past is still connected with the feeling of the present, since language has passed through the sensations of earlier generations and has preserved their inspiration" (441). To speak is to summon an entire history of usage. Words are the tradition of their applica-

13. Maurice Merleau-Ponty comments: "It is certainly right to condemn formalism, but it is ordinarily forgotten that its error is not that it esteems form too much, but that it esteems it so little that it detaches it from meaning" (*Signs*, 77).

14. See Voloshinov's discussion of Humboldt in *Marxism and the Philosophy of Language*, 45–52.

tion: they preserve the occasion and subject matter of specific occasions of utterance. The historical world leaves an indelible mark on the word, so that language cannot be understood if divorced from what it says.

A related way of thinking of language as process and event is by analogy to Austin's now-familiar speech act theory. This theory provides an analogue to Gadamer's conception of language as image insofar as it holds that the expression belongs to and is indivisible from the expressed. Speech act theory emphasizes the event of utterance, for not just the expression but also the expressing is essential. The locutionary act of utterance does not merely refer to but is itself the illocutionary act. Under certain conditions, to say "I thee wed" is to wed. There can be no langue/parole distinction in this instance, no Platonic differentiation of the thing itself and its appearance. Whereas in Plato's conception of language as number, as Gadamer points out, "being expressed, and thus bound to language, is quite secondary to the [logos]" (412), for Austin, just the opposite is true: the act of saying is not incidental but essential to what is said.

As already noted, Gadamer too argues that the appearance is not incidental to the thing (that the performance is indivisible from the symphony), so it is not surprising that his view of language as event coincides to some extent with Austin's performativism. Yet the differences are no less patent, and they come to a head in the notion of speech *act*—language as act, language as the deed of the speaking subject—where Gadamer parts ways with Austin. For Gadamer, speech act theory smacks too much of instrumentalism and its untenable asssumptions that the speaking subject *uses* signs to "do things" and that consciousness is prior to language. Gadamer's conception of language as event expresses his denial of both these assumptions. First, according to his conception, the event character of language consists in its not being the act of a subject but rather a passion, an event that happens to the subject. The subject participates in the event of Sprache, no doubt, but not as an actor or agent.

The agent of the symphony is the symphony itself; the musicians just play it. Second, in Gadamer's opinion the world does not exist prior to the word, because the word is the appearance of world, its own appearance. The language-event is not the act of the subject. This point speaks directly to the main thesis under consideration here: the word is like an image. An image is to be explained by appeal not to the person who sees it but to that which it reflects. Likewise, the word-image is an appearance not of the subject but of what is said. Speech is an event of world. "Here it really is true to say that this event is not our action upon the thing, but the act of the thing itself" (463).

Leaving aside the fact that by "Sprache" Gadamer does not mean an expression of the subject, the act of locution, or the execution of pre-given rules, his emphasis on the significance of the speech-event seemingly makes his conception of language vulnerable to the charge of logocentrism. Since Derrida too calls into question the notion of sign, and especially linguistic sign, no simple contrast can be drawn between him and Gadamer in this respect—or, as we will see, in some others.[15] Yet by asserting the primacy of writing (in a certain sense) over speech, Derrida finds himself in uneasy league with Plato and a certain strand of scientism. "The practice of scientific language," according to Derrida, "challenges intrinsically and with increasing profundity the ideal of phonetic [that is, alphabetic] writing and all its implicit metaphysics" (Of Grammatology, 10). By the same token, though, the practice of phonetic writing challenges the idea of scientific symbolism, and all its metaphysics as well. Phonetic writing indicates the indivisibility of the saying from the said, the event of language from what appears in it. Phonetic writing symbolizes the inalienability of history from meaning and the

15. In the encounter between Gadamer and Derrida, it is much to be regretted that, as Donald Marshall observes, "the encounter never took place" (Michelfelder and Palmer, Dialogue and Deconstruction, 208).

meant. Nonphonetic, unutterable writing such as mathematical symbols divide them and thereby posit a transcendental signified, the meaning per se, or what logicians sometimes call the statement or proposition. If a proposition is logically defined as the common semantic denominator of a class of synonymous sentences,[16] then it is divisible from every sentence and therefore ineffable. Conceived as proposition, the meaning of any sentence cannot as such be uttered and is perfectly ideal. Phonetic writing gives the lie to this Platonism, in that it emphasizes the fact that history (the speech-event) is inalienable from what is meant even when it is unspoken (that is, when it is written). The "Idea" is not behind, beneath, or beyond but always here and now. For Gadamer, Christianity was decisive in showing that meaning appears, in history—that the event of appearance is not incidental but belongs to what appears: "If the Word became flesh and if it is only in the incarnation that spirit is fully realized, then the logos is freed from its spirituality. . . . The uniqueness of the redemptive event introduces the essence of history into Western thought, brings the phenomenon of language out of its immersion in the ideality of meaning, and offers it to philosophical reflection. For, in contrast to the Greek logos, the word is pure event" (*Truth and Method*, 419). The infinite logos is not sullied when it appears in finite history. Instead, it is realized and fulfilled; it becomes itself more fully.[17]

Language is not just form, then, insofar as it is event. But if it is not an act, what kind of event is it? The contrast to instrumentalism is again of help. We say that we "find the right word" as if there were a

16. See Alonzo Church, "Propositions," *Encyclopedia Britannica* (1971), 18: 640, and Paul Marhenke, "The Criterion of Significance," in *Semantics and the Philosophy of Language*, ed. L. Linsky, (Urbana: University of Illinois Press, 1952), p. 146, both cited in Hirsch, *Aims of Interpretation*, 162n.

17. Ricoeur is saying something very similar in the following: "If all discourse is actualized as an event, all discourse is understood as meaning" (*Interpretation Theory*, 12).

lexical pool from which the speaker chooses appropriate semiotic vehicles. This view ignores the fact that finding the word is itself finding the thing. Even if this were not the case, however, instrumentalism would still be inadequate, for it implies that after using the verbal tool, the speaker puts it back in the same condition in which it was originally found. (This must be the case if synchronic linguistics is to be anything more than a convenient fiction, and it certainly need not be). If language is not a tool insofar as it is not a means at the disposal of the signifying subject, it is also not a tool insofar as it changes in the process of being used. "It is obvious," according to Gadamer,

> that an instrumentalist theory of signs which sees words and concepts as handy tools has missed the point of the hermeneutical phenomenon. If we stick to what takes place in speech and, above all, in every dialogue with tradition carried on by the human sciences, we cannot fail to see that here concepts are constantly in the process of being formed. This does not mean that the interpreter is using new or unusual words. But the capacity to use familiar words is not based on an act of logical subsumption, through which a particular is placed under a universal concept. Let us remember, rather, that understanding always includes an element of application and thus produces an ongoing process of concept formation. [403]

The synchronic understanding of language as a lexical pool, set of grammatical rules, network of differences, or fixed form reflects a real fact: that language exists prior to every speaker and eludes the speaker's power to change it. It does not, however, take account of the fact of metaphor. As discussed in chapter 4, metaphoric transference is not limited to identifiable rhetorical figures. It occurs whenever the same word is applied to different things. Applying it to something new and different does not leave the word unchanged, although it is still the same word. Each particular to which words are applied leaves its trace behind, and this accounts for the fact that language is constantly in the process of being not just used but created. As Gadamer explains,

> A person who speaks—who, that is to say, uses the general meanings of words—is so oriented toward the particularity of what he is perceiving that everything he says acquires a share in the particularity of the circumstances he is considering. But that means . . . that the general concept meant by the word is enriched by any given perception of a thing, so that what emerges is a new, more specific word formation. . . . However certainly speaking implies using pre-established words with general meanings, at the same time a constant process of concept formation is going on, by means of which the life of a language develops. [428–29]

Language grows, that is to say, and new concepts are formed as words are applied to new circumstances in new times. Language is no fixed form but rather an *energia*, as Humboldt called it; no instrument, because it is ceaselessly produced in being used; and no prison house but instead essentially unlimited in its capacity for recreating and renovating itself by opening itself to the different. And the engine of language's creativity, so to speak, is history—that is, the particular event and the particulars that appear in language in that event. Just as a law evolves in being applied to unforeseen cases, words evolve as well in presenting new states of affairs. That is the source of the energia of language: the historical event in which the concrete particular—the unsubsumable special case—interprets itself. It brings itself forth in language that must be new if the unique and hitherto unfamiliar is to present itself in it and yet must be old and familiar if it is to be understandable, if it is to be language at all. "The unfolding of human life in time has its own productivity," Gadamer observes (202). The multiplicity in which history unfolds itself is not "a mere fall from true unity and not a loss of home" (435) but the continuous explication, the self-interpretation, of being.

If "in language the order and structure of our experience itself is originally formed and constantly changed" and therefore "the structure of being is not simply reflected" in language (457), why does Gadamer insist that a word is almost like an image? In this context he speaks of the "speculative element" of the word,[18] where "speculation" refers to mirroring: "When something is reflected in something else, say, the castle in the lake, it means that the lake throws back the image of the castle. The mirror image is essentially connected with the actual sight of the thing through the medium of the observer. It has no being of its own; it is like an 'appearance' that is not itself and yet allows the thing to appear by means of a mirror image. It is like a duplication that is still only the one thing" (466). The image is not the thing, and words are not the things they mean. The difference is indisputable. Yet the image is of the castle and belongs to it. The reflection is the castle's own image and is inseparable from it, as words are inseparable from world. The two are indivisible, and hence one. Two, yet one: in this sense it can be said that the word is an image of that which is understood.

To understand is to interpret, to *say* what one understands, or more precisely, to participate in the event in which the understood interprets itself in language. I began by noting that interpretation as such comprehends a principle of both correctness and creativity vis-à-vis the text. That (as is now evident) is because interpretation is the self-wording of what is understood, and the speculative word and what it images (the interpretation and what interprets itself in it) are both two and one. Gadamer expresses it thus:

> The paradox that is true of all traditionary material, namely of being one and the same and yet of being different, proves that all interpretation is, in fact, speculative. Hence hermeneutics has to see through the dogmatism of a "meaning-in-itself". . . . This is what emerges from the linguistic nature of interpreta-

18. Kathleen Wright has analyzed this aspect of *Truth and Method* in detail in "Gadamer: The Speculative Structure of Language."

tion. For the interpreting word is the word of the interpreter; it is not the language and the dictionary of the interpreted text. This means that assimilation is no mere reproduction or repetition of the traditionary text. . . . The interpretation that reveals the implications of a text's meaning and brings it into language seems, when compared with the text, to be a new creation, but yet does not maintain any proper existence apart from the understanding process. [473]

To interpret is not to copy but to create something new; and yet this new interpretation is "nothing but" the understanding of the text itself. The text itself realizes itself through the occasion of its appearance, its history, the interpretive event in which it comes more fully to be.

What is it that the word-image "reflects"? With what is it both one and two? It is not given entities, according to Gadamer, or the structure of being as described by the sciences: "Every word causes the whole of the language to which it belongs to resonate and the whole worldview that underlies it to appear. . . . Thus every word, as the [finite] event of a moment, carries with it the unsaid, to which it is related by responding [to a past] and summoning [a future]. . . . There is laid up within it an infinity of meaning to be explicated and laid out" (458). This infinity is never explicit, never an intention, but rather a possibility of explication. "To say what one means . . . means to hold what is said together with an infinity of what is not said in one unified meaning and to ensure that it is understood in this way. Someone who speaks in this way may well use only the most ordinary and common words and still be able to express what is unsaid and is to be said. Someone who speaks is behaving speculatively when his words do not reflect beings, but express a relation to the whole of being" (469). The reality beyond every individual consciousness becomes visible in language, for in language not just subjective intentions but being, the totality of the unsaid together with the said, is expressed in every word. In this respect Gadamer exhibits a real affinity with Saussure, for neither of them believes that individual words reflect individual things. Even in Saussure, however, Fredric Jameson finds traces of the reflection theory of language we have been examining in Gadamer: "It is not so much the individual word or sentence that 'stands for' or 'reflects' the individual object or event in the real world, but rather that the entire system of signs, the entire field of the *langue*, lies parallel to reality itself; . . . it is the totality of systematic language, in other words, which is analogous to whatever organized structures exist in the world of reality" (*Prison-House of Language*, 32–33). Every word resonates with the whole of language, and language reflects not things but the nonfinite whole of being.

"Being that can be understood is language" means not only that language is the image of being—that language reflects being—but also that being reflects *itself* in language. That is to say, being is itself *and* its image (its reflection, but also its picture, and hence an autonomous being), and therefore not in-itself at all. This scandalizes Derrida: that being is not divisible from its image means that it *is* divisible from itself—that is, self-divided, disintegral, incoherent. "Representation mingles with what it represents," he writes. "In this play of representation, the point of origin becomes ungraspable. There are things like reflecting pools, and images, an infinite reference from one to the other, but no longer a source, a spring. There is no longer a simple origin. For what is reflected is split *in itself* and not only as an addition to itself of its image. The reflection, the image, the double, splits what it doubles. The origin of the speculation becomes a difference" (*Of Grammatology*, 36). For Derrida, then, being is split in itself, self-different. With this, Gadamer is in complete accord. His whole hermeneutics tends toward this conclusion, for it is intended to answer the impossibly simple question, What must be the nature of interpretable (understandable) being such that there are interpretations that are different from it and yet belong to it (that is, are right)? If right interpretations exist, it must be that understandable being is itself different from itself. From Gadamer's perspective, de Man is perfectly justified in describing his deconstructive reading of Proust in terms that seem to betray the most naive realism: "The reading is not 'our' reading," de Man writes. "The deconstruction is not something we have added to the text but it constituted the text in the first place" (*Allegories of Reading*, 17). The interpretation, even (and perhaps especially) the deconstructive anti-interpretation, is the text's own reflection.

This observation by Gadamer must hold universally: "It is not peculiar to the work of art that it has its being in its presentation" (*Truth and Method*, 476). Anything that presents itself, images itself, is self-divided. It is itself *and* its understandings. The nature of anything that can be understood, anything interpretable, is to present itself differently—in interpretations (not copies). Those differences are not to be understood as mistakes to be decried or forgiven. Right interpretations are *of* the thing and for that reason are *its* interpretations, and difference belongs to the thing interpreted and not just its interpreters or interpretations. Self-difference belongs to all being that can be understood.

Derrida draws the Gadamerian conclusion that there is no thing in itself because "the thing itself is a sign," and this dissolution of the transcendental signified into an endless network of signifiers, Derrida infers, amounts to "ruining the notion of the sign" (*Of Grammatology*, 50–51), for if there is no ontological difference between signifiers and signifieds, the notion of the sign based on that difference dissolves. What Derrida does not acknowledge is that once we say the thing itself is a sign, then the sign is not necessarily a sign of something other but of the thing itself. The sign becomes image.

Derrida explains only half of what needs explaining—namely, the pole of creativity, of play, the irreducible difference of the interpretation from the interpreted and of the interpreted from itself. Gadamer, however, insists on the possibility of right interpretation as well, interpretation that belongs to the thing it interprets. He does not view the self-difference of being as a scandal, a hidden worm eating out the heart of being. Rewriting Heidegger's conclusion that the meaning of being is time, Gadamer's first and last insight is "that being is self-presentation and that all understanding is an event [of being]" (*Truth and Method*, 484). Being "is" the events in which it presents itself, its appearances, its images, its interpretations, its language. Being, then, is two: self-divided, as Derrida insists. But these are *its* images, *its* appearances, *its* language. Being, then, is one. At this point, Gadamer parts ways with Derrida, for to Gadamer language is image, and it not only splits what it reflects but also holds it in unity:

> That which can be understood is language. This means that it is of such a nature that of itself it offers itself to be understood. Here too is confirmed the speculative structure of language. To come into language does not mean that a second being is acquired. Rather, what something presents itself as belongs to its own being. Thus everything that is language has a speculative unity: it contains a distinction, that between its being and its presentations of itself, but this is a distinction that is really not a distinction at all. [475]

A word, an event, anything that can be understood, is a sign, no doubt. It contains a difference between what it is and what it means, its being and its interpretation. And yet it is not just a sign but something like an image. For if right interpretation is possible, if all difference and plurality is not mere mistake, if the history of interpretations is not to be explained as an accident of errant subjectivity, then some difference must be intrinsic to the thing understood. Some interpretations must reflect the thing's own self-difference, and the plurality of right interpretations therefore must be events in the history, the self-differing, the self-interpretation of the interpreted "itself."

6

THE QUESTION OF

THE CLASSIC

"To call any work of art 'classical,' implies either the highest praise or the most contemptuous abuse, according to the party to which one belongs." Thus T. S. Eliot described the situation of the classic nearly a half-century ago—factionalized, partisan, extreme (*On Poetry and Poets*, 53). Our time too seems unpropitious for thinking about the question of the classic, for once again it seems to be a simple either/or that requires merely a choosing of sides: for or against? back to the classics or away from them? Our time calls not for thinking but a vote. And it may well be too late for thinking about the classic in any case, for the vote is already in, and the nays have it. Admittedly, an isolated few who profess the classics still remain—noble and pathetic warriors who fight on, unaware that the war is over. But their persistence does not alter the fact. The new battle of the ancients and moderns had the same victor as the old one, and the vanquished can only exclaim *O tempora! O mores!* and wonder *ubi sunt.*

Of course this is an exaggeration, at most only half of the story. Even if Robert von Hallberg is right that among academics there has emerged a new orthodoxy of suspicion about the classic (*Canons*, 1), this consensus scarcely includes the public or even some notable public officials. The time is past when the defenders of the classics were automatically to be found within the academy and their detractors found without—in church or state or both. Now the case is very nearly the reverse. "Something peculiar has been happening lately to the classics," Lawrence Lipking observes ("Aristotle's Sister," 103) and it is of a piece with what is happening to liberalism generally and liberal education in particular. So far are we from being able to reclaim the legacy, to recall William Bennett's phrase, it is difficult even to remember what liberal education was supposed to be. But if, with Leo Strauss, we think of it simply as "studying with proper care the great books which the greatest minds have left behind" (*Liberalism*, 3), then it is evident that the classics must fall under the same indictment as the education that transmits them: liberal education, simply put, has come to be regarded by many as fundamentally illiberal.

Mary O'Brien, for example, conceives of "education as a mode of social control . . . dedicated to the justification of the present by the past" ("Feminism," 93). "The 'new' Right," she argues, "is, in a number of ways, 'old' liberalism" (97), and it follows that what used to be called "liberal education is essentially a mode of conservation" (102). What it conserves is ultimately the repressive tradition, and mediately the classics that underwrite it. Thus, those who hope to rechannel the tradition must, in Christine Froula's words, "transform a pedagogy which conceived 'Great Books' on the model of sacred texts into one which calls into question the unexamined hierarchies invoked by the Arnoldian ideal, 'the acquainting ourselves with the best that has been thought and said in the world'" ("When Eve Reads Milton," 171). Among others, the Syracuse University English Department has begun this transformation, and its collectively written manifesto announces that "the end of an education in literature will be, not the traditional 'well read' student, but a student capable of critique: of actively pressuring, resisting and questioning cultural texts" (Cohan et al., "Not a Good Idea," 2).

Given this revaluation, the academics and the politicians seem to concur on the fact of the matter. Neither O'Brien nor Froula nor the Syracuse English Department would differ substantially with William Bennett's conclusion that "humanities education is no longer an introduction to, and immersion in, the best that has been thought and known"; nor would Bennett arouse much disagreement when he describes the aim of liberal education as liberation: "the cultivation of free men and women" ("Shattered Humanities"). But the very classics that Bennett celebrates as the key to emancipation, oppositional academics decry as the prison itself. Thus, while both agree that there has been a shift from cultural bequest to cultural critique, Bennett regards academic skepticism about the classics as a treason of the clerks, whereas the clerks themselves view it as opening up a brave new world—a world of difference without domination, plurality without hierarchy.

This is a world that has no place for the classics, only for texts, and all texts are created equal. "*No text* is so trivial as to be outside the bounds of humanistic study," Robert Scholes declares. "The meanest graffito, if fully understood in its context, can be a treasure of human expressiveness" ("Aiming a Canon," 116). Scholes's textbook (appropriately titled *Text Book*) includes no classics, only texts, and those are underwritten by the democratic principle: "the theory that informs this book has led us to present literature in a democratic way—not as a set of untouchable great works."[1] Such democracy is incompatible with greatness—or with the greatness of great books, at least, for it may well seem that greatness has not been eliminated but rather surreptitiously transferred to the critics.

The egalitarian shift toward unhierarchized textuality undoubtedly invites us to a salutary broadening of our sympathies to include the literature of women, minorities, and emergent nations—as well

---

1. "Instructor's Manual," in Scholes, Comley, and Ulmer, *Text Book*, iii. In *Textual Power*, Scholes voices some suspicion of "the egalitarian impulse" (77), but he offers no principle of hierarchy to resist it.

as graffiti. One can applaud the expansive embrace of the new romanticism while still realizing that something is amiss: the universalization of textuality represents a reassertion of the global ambitions of literature. By "substituting the concept of *text* for the traditional concept of *literature*," *Text Book* "allows for the presentation of a wider range of material and a broader spectrum of approaches to literary study. . . . This is an inclusive, not an exclusive approach" (V). The old formalists might object that when nothing is excluded from literature, nothing is left of literature; but by a curious reversal we can see that just the opposite is also the case. For when nothing is excluded, literature (now called "text") becomes an all-inclusive category. The universe becomes a universe of discourse, the world is textualized, literaturized, and the literature professors reclaim their lost empire. Though literature had sadly degenerated into an optional specialization, a major among majors, now as "text" it once again regains its rightful place as universal and foundational, a master category, a mandatory path—even a required course—on the way to knowledge.

The new textual "transdisciplinarity"—textual analysis of philosophical texts, legal texts, historical texts, and many things that are not verbal texts at all—in fact manifests a disciplinary self-aggrandizement that might well give us pause. In certain respects, pantextualism has merely universalized the puristic aestheticism from which we were fleeing insofar as it acknowledges no Other of the text, no non-text to puncture its pretensions to universality and resist its imperialist ambitions. When Froula recommends a pedagogy of interrogation that "calls into question" the best that has been thought and said, when the Syracuse English Department aims to educate students in "resisting and questioning cultural texts," when Scholes views wisdom "not as something transmitted from the text to the student but as something developed in the student by questioning the text" (*Textual Power*, 14), we begin to wonder whether despite all this questioning some questions are nevertheless precluded—indeed precisely the ones that would call the authority of the questioner into question.

"I want the right as a teacher to study and teach every text critically," Scholes asserts against Bennett. "To be told that I must teach *any* text in a reverent manner would be to drain the very life blood from my practice as a teacher" ("Aiming a Canon," 115). Who among us does not sympathize with such resistance to enforced reverence, whether the force is governmental or traditional? "Prescriptive veneration" (as Samuel Johnson termed it) seems the very antithesis of critical thought. Yet it is not difficult to see that just such veneration is a condition of self-criticism, for "those who esteem and revere are therefore not self-satisfied."[2] What texts does the pantextualist reverence?[3] If there are some, are they properly called "texts," or might they better be termed "scripture"? And if there are not, how does critical thought that venerates no text escape venerating itself and thus becoming uncritical?

The consequence of leveling the classic with the graffito is that questioning becomes unilateral. Interpretation becomes essentially interrogation or inquisition, for the difference between a graffito and a classic is this: the graffito doesn't talk back. Text is patient of construction. Like verbal tofu, it submits passively to critical processing of every description. The classic too is undeniably subject to critique. That one cannot have done critiquing it is in part what makes it a classic. It is not, however, merely an object of criticism precisely insofar as it has the capacity to criticize the critic. Not William Bennett but the classic itself is what must be denied in order to exercise the right to teach every text critically, for the classic is

2. The phrase is Allan Bloom's. See *The Closing of the American Mind* (New York: Simon and Schuster, 1987), p. 195.

3. In *Textual Power* Scholes claims that "the worst thing we can do is to foster in [students] an attitude of reverence before texts" (16). Scholes acknowledges the need, as I do, for something that would qualify as non-text (86–110). But for him it is the referent (i.e, the world), not a scripture (i.e., a work worthy of reverence).

what calls into question the omnipotence of critical reflection. The classic not only submits to questioning but turns to interrogate its inquisitors—if they are willing to listen. Hegel underscores this reversal when he says that the classic "is essentially a question, an address to the responsive breast, a call to the mind and the spirit" (*Aesthetics*,1:71).[4]

This hardly settles the matter, but it does open it up. If we consider the classic as making a statement—or, more radically, all classics as making the same statement—then the classic is the object of a referendum: it demands that we take a stand, make a commitment. But if Hegel is right, if the classic is not just a statement but a question addressed to the critic, then what is required is not only a referendum but a dialogue. There are two questions involved: the question (suspicious or otherwise) that the interpreter addresses to the work and the question that the work addresses to the interpreter. Such reciprocity of response is the condition of any genuine democracy. The full process of interpreting the classic consists in a reciprocal questioning, a dialogue whereby the interpreter too becomes the interpreted. The question of the classic in this respect is how to keep the dialogue going.

In what follows, my intent is not so much to provide a series of definitions, or defend a series of theses, as to open up further questions raised by the classic with the aim of restoring reciprocity, giving both partners in the dialogue their due, and preventing either from being silenced.

THE CLASSICAL AS CHALLENGE TO THE CANONICAL

One way the classic has recently been silenced is by being subsumed under the idea of the canon. To be sure, the two ideas

4. Hegel actually says it is the work of art which is essentially a question. For reasons that will appear below, I have altered "work of art" to "the classic."

overlap to a considerable extent. In many contexts "the classics" and "the canon" refer to the same works, and any attempt to dichotomize them would be misleading. Nevertheless, "the classic" is not always synonymous with "the canonical," and differentiating them may help us see more exactly how they fit together.[5]

The asymmetrical grammar of the two terms offers a clue to their semantic differences. First, "canon" is a collective noun denominating a group of works with a common author or authority. There is, however, no noun denominating an individual canonical book; all we have is the adjective. The reverse is true of the "classic." In this case, there is a noun for each work but none for the collective whole made up of all the individual classics. All we have is the plural. Second, while there is a verb "to canonize," no such verb exists to name the process whereby a classic becomes a classic. From these two asymmetries, several conclusions can be drawn about the connotations of the two terms.

For its part, the canon is essentially plural but determinate. A canon includes indefinitely many books, but however many it includes, there are still others it excludes. For the Christian, sixty-seven books compose one Bible, and the unity of The Book implies the exclusion of the aprocrypha. In regard to literature, one can say further that from the viewpoint of the excluded, the literary canon exhibits a telling ideological homogeneity—hundreds, thousands of works all with one message: members only. Conversely, viewed from within, the internal unity of the canon disappears. "The community of the greatest minds is rent by discord and even by various kinds of discord," as Leo Strauss observes (*Liberalism*, 4). The allegation that the immense diversity of the literary canon exhibits an ideological coherence, let alone homogeneity, is merely silly. Both

5. For an alternative view of the distinction between canon and classic, which came to my attention too late to be directly addressed here, see Gumbrecht, " 'Phoenix from the Ashes.' "

viewpoints may well be right, and they are certainly not contradictory.

While the canon is plural but determinate, grammatical usage suggests that "the classic," by contrast, is essentially singular but indeterminate. Commensurate with the idea of the classic, unlike that of the canon, is the possibility that there are not many classics but in fact only one—what Eliot called the "absolute" classic, which for him was Virgil (*On Poetry and Poets*, 68). But Eliot spoke of "relative" classics as well—classics of a certain language, genre, or period—and of these there can be as many as one pleases. Every class of works can have its classic, and since the class of classes is essentially unlimited, so also is the class of classics. If the motto of the canon is *e pluribus unum*, that of the classic is *aut unum aut infinitum*. Given this potential limitlessness, the classic is a more generous and capacious, less exclusionary notion than the canon. "I believe the Temple of Taste needs to be remodeled," wrote Sainte-Beuve. "Above all, I should not exclude anyone among the worthy: I want everyone so entitled to have his place there, from that greatest and least self-conscious of all the classics—Shakespeare—to the very least of the classics in miniature, to Andrieux. 'My Father's house has many mansions'—let this be true of the Kingdom of the Beautiful no less than of the Kingdom of Heaven" ("What Is a Classic?," 8).

This is not to say that everyone is admitted to either kingdom, however; and if we consider the usage of the verb "to canonize," it is apparent that while anything is canonical that has been canonized, no such process opens the doors to the Kingdom of the Classic. Rather, to gain admittance there requires inherent quality, worth, value. The particular qualities are irrelevant for our immediate purpose: the point is that, unlike the canonical, the classic as such claims intrinsic value because there is for the classic no process equivalent to canonization. Classicality is a property of the work and even its being. Both adjective and noun, classic is what a classic is. Canonicity, in contrast, is not a quality or characteristic of the work (still less its being) but rather the result of what has happened to it—namely, canonization, a process which the work undergoes and which alters nothing in it. The claim of the classic is essential; the claim of the canonical is either institutional, conventional, or historical, but in any case accidental.

Thus Barbara Herrnstein Smith convincingly argues that the value of the canonical is "radically contingent" with respect to the work canonized ("Contingencies of Value," 18). If so, canonical value invites not an investigation of intrinsic properties but the description of a process: the social dynamic that (like the religious determination) confers value on canonical literature. Whereas the naive notion of value considered it as belonging to the object, Smith takes the more sophisticated, Nietzschean view that there are no valid judgments of value, for canonical value is a product of a collective cultural subject; and cultural products (like natural effects) have no claim to validity, no truth-value. Smith's theory of value as cultural product offers the prospect of change to those who believe change is needed. This is *its* value, here and now. If the cultural and social mechanisms productive of value can be precisely understood and intentionally modified, then the destructive effects they produce might possibly be prevented. There is still hope.

Yet the one-sidedness of Smith's "canonical" view appears when she attempts to universalize its provenance. Because she equates the two, Smith extrapolates the canonical onto the classical. Thus her conception of classical value approximates that of Lord Chesterfield: "Classical knowledge," he wrote to his son, "is absolutely necessary for everybody; because everybody has agreed to think and to call it so" (*Letters*, vol. 3, no. 1564). Even if, as J. W. Johnson has shown, "everybody" means nothing more in this case than "everybody who is anybody" (*England*, 4)[6]—and it may be that such

6. See also Johnson's *Formation of English Neo-Classical Thought*, chap. 1.

conventions are always somehow limited—Chesterfield's is nevertheless a conventionalist conception of classical value, and, like Smith's, it therefore suits the canonical better than the classical. Whereas the canon is nothing but works that have been canonized—that people have agreed to call canonical—classic is what certain works are. When Smith's monistic theory of value, perfectly adequate to the canon, is expanded to universality, it does not explain the value of the classic but merely explains it away as at bottom canonical.

Smith's account is designed to explain what she takes to be "the most fundamental character of literary value, which is its mutability and diversity" ("Contingencies of Value," 17). Clearly, orthodox conventionalist theory—that is, "canonical" theory—has the advantage in explaining difference and change. Just as clearly, however, it always stumbles in explaining sameness, and here the advantage moves to the "classical" theory, which explains the permanence of value by attributing it to permanent qualities inherent in the classic. In his book *The Classic* Frank Kermode voices this essentialist position when he concludes that underlying the classic "is a substance that prevails, however powerful the agents of change" (134). Smith might well object that although there is no name for the cultural process whereby a work becomes a classic, this hardly proves that classicality is not the product of a social dynamic. And if in fact the classic consists in disguising this process behind specious metaphysical claims to enduring substance and intrinsic value, then the only difference between the classical and the canonical is that the classical is more mystified.

There is a good deal of truth to this, but it is not the whole truth. For just as the essentialist underestimates the reality of change and difference, so the analogous conventionalist move, when it comes to explaining sameness, is to deny that there is any such thing as sameness to be explained. Thus Smith makes short work of Hume: to Hume's assertion that "the same Homer who pleased at Athens two thousand years ago is still admired at Paris and London" she retorts, "It is . . . never 'the *same* Homer'" ("Contingencies of Value," 31). She does not deny that Homer is valued as today as he was two centuries or two millennia ago, but merely that the "highly variable entity we refer to as 'Homer'" contains any invariant essence that would explain the invariant estimation accorded it.

What, then, does explain the invariance? Smith answers, "The endurance of a classic canonical author such as Homer" is due to his being "enmeshed in the network of intertextuality that continuously *constitutes* the high culture of the orthodoxly educated population of the West" (34–35). The italics are Smith's, for she wishes to emphasize that the classics belong to the intertext that constitutes Western culture, Western values. The classical canon, in part at least, *constitutes* the culture. But Smith's main argument has been just the opposite, that canonical value (and therefore the canon itself) is constituted by culture. These two positions may both be correct. They are not necessarily exclusive, but they do suggest that classic and canon are involved in a dialectical process of reciprocal determination: the classical canon creates the culture that creates the canon of classics. Smith's main argument is not wrong; it is merely one-sided because it stops short. It does not move from the canonical to the classical—or, more precisely, it overemphasizes the canonical as the product of social dynamism and insufficiently acknowledges the classical as the producer and agent of that very dynamism.

If the classical is not equivalent to the canonical, neither are the two dichotomous; they are twin aspects of one circle. There is no need to posit Western culture as a permanent and homogeneous complex of values and thus deny its self-difference; culture maintains itself by changing. There is also no need to affirm that Homer is always different, and thus deny the classic its identity. Neither always the same nor always different, the classic embodies the problem, in Frank Kermode's terms, of the "relations between the enduring and the transient, the essence and the disposition" (*The Classic,*

44). But just as Kermode errs on the side of enduring, the "substance that prevails," so Smith errs on the side of the transient. Each reflecting a half-truth, neither Kermode's essentialism nor Smith's conventionalism is wholly satisfying, for the classic is *alter et idem*. Precisely this is what Gadamer means by asserting that "the classic epitomizes a general characteristic of historical being" (*Truth and Method*, 289)—namely, that historical being is the kind of being which, precisely by altering, comes into its own and thus is irreducibly both other and itself. Conceived in this way, the question of the classic and of history itself is how to think unity and plurality, sameness and difference, without denying either.

SAMENESS AND CONTINUITY

Histories of the classical often begin with Aulus Gellius, who in the second century A.D. distinguished the *classicus scriptor* from the *proletarius*. Here "classicus" designates an author from a high tax bracket, a member of the upper class as opposed to the rabble. Viewed from this perspective, the classic from its inception belongs to a socioeconomic history. In the sixth century Magnus Felix Ennodius termed a student who attends classes as a "classicus," and Pierre Littré, the nineteenth-century French lexicographer, defined the *classique* as that which is taught in classes (hardly a ridiculous definition).[7] Here the classic belongs to an institutional history. And yet, in a sense that will need to be explained, the classics do not simply belong to history but also make history. Alive and dead, they are not just historical but historic and history-producing.

Temporal distance, one aspect of the historical, is frequently taken as a defining characteristic of the classic, and I will so consider it here; but it is, in fact, not the only or even a necessary characteristic.

7. For the facts cited in this paragraph, see Fleischmann, "Classicism."

The idea of the classic consists of three strands variously inter-
twined. First, the classic is an undefined demand. "Speaking our
own language and governed by the conditions of the age in which we
find ourselves," Sainte-Beuve writes, "let us ask ourselves from time
to time, . . . our eyes on the group of mortals we most revere: 'What
would they say of us?'" ("What Is a Classic?," 10). Sainte-Beuve had
no doubt that the revered classics do have something to say about us,
and though what they say is not entirely clear, it is rather discomfit-
ing. Greatness invites invidious comparison. The classic instills in its
reader a general and unlocalized sense of inadequacy, implying an
unspecified obligation. The classic makes demands of its readers,
then, but they are intrinsically vague and are specified (if at all) only
variously—from reader to reader or time to time. Second, at those
times when the claim of the classic on every reader is particularized,
when the "greatness" of the great book is concretized in a specific
standard or rule, then the classical becomes identified with particular traits, namely, those qualities of works that explain their quality
and that ought therefore to be emulated. The classic is not just a
particular book but a type or prototype, an imitable, repeatable set
of formal features and thematic values—such as T. E. Hulme's "hard
dryness" ("Classicism and Romanticism," 126). Whatever specific
traits are regarded as defining the classic, they can be embodied in
modern works as well; at any time any work that has them is
classical. But, third, if the classic works that possess these valued
characteristics appear grouped together in a specific time, the classic
comes to denote a period; and since this is almost invariably a
remote period, temporal distance typically comes to define the classic. If "it is *only* by hindsight," as Eliot says, "that a classic can be
known as such" (*On Poetry and Poets*, 3; italics added), that is
because the classic has no distinguishing characteristics that enable
one to recognize it in the contemporary. Nothing modern, but anything at all that is ancient and still valued, can be a classic, regardless
of its specific qualities. Thus the classic comes to be inextricable
from a sense of time, history, and the past.

Pope called into question what had been up until his day the standard conception of the classic in relation to time. The Horatian tradition required a hundred years of the classic, and given this test, it seemed that time of itself confers value. In "To Augustus" Pope the modern asks his Horatian interlocutor the essential questions:

> If Time improve our Wit as well as Wine,
> Say at what age a Poet grows divine?
> Shall we, or shall we not, account him so,
> Who dy'd, perhaps, an hundred years ago?
> End all dispute; and fix the year precise
> When British bards begin t'Immortalize?
>   "Who lasts a Century can have no flaw,
> I hold that Wit a Classick, good in law."
>   Suppose he wants a year, will you compound?
> And shall we deem him Ancient, right and sound,
> Or damn him to all Eternity at once,
> At ninety nine, a Modern, and a Dunce?
>   "We shall not quarrel for a year or two;
> By courtesy of England, he may do."
>   Then, by the rule that made the Horse-tail bare,
> I pluck out year by year, as hair by hair,
> And melt down Ancients like a heap of snow:
> While you, to measure merits, look in Stowe,
> And estimating Authors by the year,
> Bestow a Garland on a Bier. [*Poems*, 637]

Pope's is a self-serving argument, of course, but his objections are still well taken. The point at which quantity becomes quality, at which the temporal distance is sufficient to consecrate a given work as a classic, is entirely undeterminable: a century is just as arbitrary a measure of classicality as a generation or a year. No distance is ipso facto so short as to disqualify a work from classical status; and by the same argument no distance is long enough to render that judgment definitive.

Even though Pope rejects the hundred-year test, his "Horse-tail" argument relies on the same conception of time as does that of his Horatian opponent. Both regard time as fluid, infinitely divisible, and continuous, and this notion of time has for its correlate the analogous notion of a continuously enduring classic, ever one and the same. "The idea of the classical," Sainte-Beuve writes, "implies continuity and consistency, a tradition that forms a whole, is handed down, and endures ("What Is a Classic?," 3). Defined by appeal to uninterrupted continuity, the classic is that which lasts not just because of the passage of time but also despite it. Improbable endurance amid the ruins of time constitutes the value of the classic. The surviving works of Aeschylus and Sophocles, Sainte-Beuve writes, "remind us of others, who deserved no doubt to survive as much as they, but who succumbed to the ravages of time. This alone should teach us not to oversimplify our view of literature, even of classical literature. We should recognize that the order which has prevailed for so long, which is so exact and well-proportioned, is a highly artificial creation, based on our limited knowledge of the past" (5). Survival explains value, according to Sainte-Beuve, not the reverse.

In time, death is the rule, but the deathless classics that are the exception reflect the seamless continuity of time itself. Eliot conceives that continuity organically, in terms of growth and ripeness. "A classic," he asserts, "can only occur when a civilization is mature; when a language and a literature are mature," and a poet "cannot bring that language to maturity unless the work of his predecessors has prepared it for his final touch. A mature literature, therefore, has a history behind it" (*On Poetry and Poets*, 55). Eliot is here defending Virgil as absolute classic, and thus must explain Virgil's predecessors as prefigurations in a history leading up to the *Aeneid*. From an alternative (say, Homeric) point of view, the classic does not trail a history behind it but rather prophetically projects a history before it. From the Virgilian point of view, the classic is the mature fruit for which its predecessors prepared; but the classic is also the seed that generates a line of successors and thus initiates a history. In either case, in retrospect or prospect, the advent of the classic is not just historical but is a historic event. It gathers a history to it, organizes and unifies history. The classic makes history and thus is not merely the object of historical research but also its condition. The locus of unity in diversity, the classic is the still point of sameness and continuity in the succession of generations.

Within this continuity, moreover, the classic is what is handed down in tradition, the substance of the legacy. All who inherit it, however remote, are thereby united with each other, as well as dissociated from the disenfranchised. At the famous dinner party arranged by Boswell and recounted in his biography of Johnson, John Wilkes objected to citing the classics in conversation as pedantic. But Johnson replied, "No, Sir, it is a good thing; there is a community of mind in it. Classical quotation is the *parole* of literary men all over the world" (1143).[8] What Johnson means by "parole" is precisely not what Saussure means by it, and in fact his usage calls Saussure's very distinction between langue and parole into question. The classics, concrete acts of speech, are also themselves a language. The classically literate "speak" the classics and thereby recognize and communicate with one another. Simultaneously form and content, the classics ground a community of mind.

With respect to literary judgment, the community of mind embodied in the classic defines the standard of taste. "What we find in a period of classic prose," Eliot observes, "is a community of taste" (*On Poetry and Poets*, 57). Kant opens up larger questions of community when he calls taste the only true common sense, defined as

8. Concerning implicit reference to shared knowledge, Todorov writes that it "imposes *complicity* on the interlocutors. It is because they have a common collective memory and belong to the same social group that they can understand each other. The affirmation of this complicity may even be the only real goal of such an indirect evocation" (*Symbolism and Interpretation*, 69).

the ability to make our feeling in a given presentation "*universally communicable*, without the mediation of a concept" (*Critique of Judgment*, 138). But not merely aesthetic feeling is at issue in the question of the classic, considered in the context of common sense. A classic that possesses high literary merit may well be more valuable for its aesthetic qualities, but it is no more a classic for them. The range of classics extends beyond art, to history and philosophy, and beyond the liberal arts to classics of science and of all other kinds. If classics of every kind embody the common standard of taste, then the *sensus communis* is not restricted to universally communicable aesthetic feelings but has a cognitive provenance as well. The universe of the classic comprehends everything shared and common, everything that is intelligible without the need for explanation, everything that is assumed as apparent and indisputable, everything upon which further thought can be based. The classics not only ground a sense of community but are the locus of common sense.

Like Chesterfield, we can therefore infer that everyone who wants this common sense, everybody who would belong to this community, needs to know the classics. Yet the need to know them does not necessarily mean everyone needs to read them. E. D. Hirsch is quite right that cultural literacy necessitates no particular canon, no list of great books whatever, for what they contain can be gotten from a great many other places besides the books themselves.[9] More frequently than firsthand, the classics are read secondhand, thirdhand, or hundredth-hand. Everyone can be—and to some degree, in fact, always is—classically literate without having read the classics at all. The classical legacy is a bequest the heirs cannot reject, for they have always already inherited the classics even before having read them.

As the origin of common sense, or as a language one has acquired

9. See *Cultural Literacy*, xiv, and "'Cultural Literacy' Does Not Mean 'Canon.'"

prior to the consciousness of having done so, the classics are the common medium of thought. Thus (as medium) they both prevent all immediate intuition and enable all mediate cognition. In eighteenth-century terms, the classics are the locus of prejudice. "Illustrious examples," Edward Young claimed, "prejudice our judgment in favour of their abilities, and so lessen the sense of our own; and they intimidate us with the splendor of their renown, and thus under diffidence bury our strength" (*Conjectures*, 17). Although the classics restrict self-assurance and disable individual thought, as Young indicates, they manifest the enabling and liberating function of prejudice as well. Burke is usually cited in this context, but consider the opinion of Winckelmann, who comes to much the same conclusion as Burke: "The authority of antiquity predetermines our judgments; yet even this prepossession has been not without its advantages; for he who always proposes to himself to *find much* will by *seeking* for much perceive something" (*Ancient Art*, 3/4:365). For Winckelmann, a prejudice in favor of the classics is the necessary condition for perceiving anything at all in them.

These antithetical conceptions of the effect of prejudice correspond to two equally opposed conceptions of the ends of education. Allan Bloom voices the orthodox Enlightenment view when he says, "No real teacher can doubt that his task is to assist his pupil to fulfill human nature against all the deforming forces of convention and prejudice" (*Closing of the American Mind*, 20). And yet in a complete volte-face Bloom expresses the classical Burkean view of prejudice as well: "When I was a young teacher at Cornell, I once had a debate about education with a professor of psychology. He said that it was his function to get rid of prejudices in his students. . . . Did this professor know what those prejudices meant for the students and what effect being deprived of them would have? . . . I found myself responding . . . that I personally tried to teach my students prejudices" (42).

The end of education, then, is to instill prejudices or to dispel them. In either case, teaching the classics functions to acquaint students for the first time with what they have always known, to bring that foreknowledge to explicit consciousness and thus make it available for denial and affirmation. With such education students are given the freedom to share willingly in the tradition that gave them birth or to hack the aged parent to pieces. But insofar as the revolutionary alternative requires the greater authority, the father is customarily ousted in the more authoritative name of the grandfather. Thus continuity is preserved even in the midst of revolution. If one classic can only be displaced by another, continuity is in fact the condition of any change, however radical.

Especially as a communal heritage voluntarily handed down in ceremonies and institutions of conservation, and as a common sense tacitly disseminated as the self-evidence that grounds all other truths, the idea of the classic involves not only spatial community among persons but temporal continuity among generations and periods. It implies survival and endurance, an uninterrupted sameness such that the time of the classic is continuous with historian's time. Within this continuity, the classic is inalienably united to every successive present by the infinitely elastic umbilical of time.

REPETITION AND DIFFERENCE

Beginning in the mid-eighteenth century, however, there were signs that the continuity was being broken. In pursuing the idea of the classic as it metamorphosed thereafter, I cannot hope to do justice to the semantic variations among the multiple senses of the term, as these would need to be discriminated in any thoroughgoing history. Though wary of the semantic homogenization that results, I must content myself with concentrating instead on the fact of immediate interest: that when highly various authors wanted to speak, for example, of what is not romantic, or not symbolic, or not modern, all chose the word "classic." In almost every case after 1750, the classic has come to denote primarily a period, a past time now over.

The preface to Johnson's edition of Shakespeare represents one stage in the breakdown of continuity and sameness that significantly altered the idea of the classic. Johnson cites the Horatian test mentioned above, but for him the passage of time neither confers value of itself nor impedes endurance. Rather, the ravages of time are the very condition of recognizing the classic. As Johnson says,

> The Poet, of whose works I have undertaken the revision, may now begin to assume the dignity of an ancient, and claim the privilege of established fame and prescriptive veneration. He has long outlived his century, the term commonly fixed as the test of literary merit. Whatever advantages he might once derive from personal allusions, local customs, or temporary opinions, have for many years been lost; and every topick of merriment or motive of sorrow, which the modes of artificial life afforded him, now only obscure the scenes which they once illuminated. The effects of favour and competition are at an end; the tradition of his friendships and his enmities has perished; his works . . . are read without any other reason than the desire of pleasure, and are therefore praised only as pleasure is obtained. [*Johnson on Shakespeare*, 61]

In "To Augustus," as noted, Pope professes not to understand why his interlocutor should "Bestow a Garland only on a Bier." Johnson explains the reason: death abstracts the genuine from the artificial, the universal from the local, and the timeless from the temporary. What passes is not just time but the times of the author and his initial audience, and their very passing away is revelatory. "There is a kind of intellectual remoteness necessary for the comprehension of any great work in its full design and its true proportions," Johnson writes (111). Temporal distance reveals the real and true, and if no particular distance is definitive, that means only that the truth keeps on being revealed as Shakespeare accrues new honors in every generation.

Whereas conceiving the classic as a survivor within a historical continuity minimizes the possible disconnectedness of past and present, Johnson can hardly be accused of ignoring the reality of death, the archetype of all division. Nevertheless, his conception of a classic that outlives its author—whose immortality is manifested precisely by the death of the author—ultimately denies discontinuity even more resolutely than does simply ignoring it. Winckelmann, on the contrary, finds no such consoling unity with the past. His massive labor of love, the *Geschichte der Kunst des Altertums*, concludes not with the death of the Greek sculptors, painters, and architects but the death of ancient art itself, its destruction at the hands of the Romans. Winckelmann's elegiac tone therefore expresses a hopeless nostalgia:

> I could not refrain from searching into the fate of works of art as far as my eye could reach; just as a maiden, standing on the shore of the ocean, follows with tearful eyes her departing lover with no hope of ever seeing him again, and fancies that in the distant sail she sees the image of her beloved. Like that loving maiden we too have, as it were, nothing but a shadowy outline left of the object of our wishes, but that very indistinctness awakens only a more earnest longing for what we have lost.
> [*Ancient Art*, 3/4:364]

Where Johnson finds continuity amid change, Winckelmann finds simply loss and discontinuity.

For Hegel too classic art is permanently lost, and its departure is of even broader significance for him than for Winckelmann, since its passing imports the pastness of art per se. In the progress that Hegel's *Aesthetics* delineates from symbolic to classic to romantic art, it is the classical that represents "the highest pinnacle of [what] . . . art could achieve, and if there is something defective in it, the defect is just art itself and the restrictedness of the sphere of art" (79). Since the classical epitomizes the idea of art as such and since classic art has been superseded by romantic, Hegel's conclusion inevitably follows: "Art, considered in its highest vocation, is and remains for us a thing of the past. Thereby it has lost for us genuine truth and life, and has rather been transferred into our *ideas* instead of maintaining its earlier necessity in reality" (11). Art, simply stated, belongs to history.

Despite Heidegger and Gadamer's attempt to appeal Hegel's verdict, it has an inescapable currency for all neoromantics. Even if we leave open the question of art generally and confine our attention to the classic, for those who have little Latin and less Greek, who hope for genius because they cannot claim learning, the classic is assuredly a thing of the past. For us, it is situated on the far side of a barrier. Thus Foucault speaks of "the threshold that separates us from Classical thought and constitutes our modernity" (*Order of Things*, xxii). Not unlike Hegel, Foucault finds

> two great discontinuities in the *episteme* of Western culture: the first inaugurates the Classical age (roughly half-way through the seventeenth century) and the second, at the beginning of the nineteenth century, marks the beginning of the modern age. The order on the basis of which we think today does not have the same mode of being as that of the Classical thinkers. Despite the impression we may have of an almost uninterrupted development of the European *ratio* from the Renaissance to our own day, . . . all this quasi-continuity on the level of ideas and themes is doubtless only a surface appearance; on the archaeological level, we see that the system of positivities was transformed in a wholesale fashion at the end of the eighteenth and beginning of the nineteenth century. [xxii]

By Foucault's account, what ended with the end of the classic episteme was precisely not a particular period. Rather, continuity itself was interrupted, and in a certain sense at that point history began. Within continuous time, the past is never completely past, for the present always remains tethered to it; but the end of the classic provided just the finality necessary to create history as what is over. History in this sense is constitutively punctuated by discontinuous periods, *epochēs* followed by new openings, and between them nothing. The "wholesale transformation" without transition that occurs with the closure of the classical episteme demarcates past from present, ancient from modern, and thus inaugurates our epoch. Modernity is that episteme constituted by the fact that it conceives the classical only historically. Whether to be regarded with regret or condescension, it is for us a thing of the past. The classic is indeed the epitome of all things historical, estranged, academic, and dead.

Given death, the idea of an uninterrupted tradition and the corollary metaphor of a rich legacy continuously handed down lose their credibility. Eliot voices a thoroughly modern, romantic sense of the past when he says, "Tradition . . . cannot be inherited, and if you want it you must obtain it by great labour" (*Selected Essays*, 4). Exiled from the unity of undissociated tradition, romantic man must labor for intellectual sustenance. For the disinherited, culture must be cultivated. "We are . . . like poorly portioned heirs," Winckelmann too laments. "But we look carefully about us," he continues, "and by deductions from many particulars we arrive at least at a probable certainty [about the past]." Winckelmann acknowledges that the death of the classic is absolute: the maiden gazes after her departed lover "with no hope of seeing him again." Yet, he suggests, there still is a way to commune with the departed: "We are like those who wish to have an interview with spirits" (*Ancient Art*, 3/4:364–65). Access to the classical past is made possible by the seance, the "deductions from many particulars" that are historical research. Historiography and allegory are in one respect complementary: if history puts the present into contact with the classic, allegory accommodates the classic to the present. And yet it is obviously no accident that history disavows and discredits the anachronisms of allegory. Winckelmann suggests one reason why: whereas allegorical accommodation sustains what is still living, historical research retrieves what is already dead.

Brought back across the great divide by historians, the classic possesses no continuity of sameness with them. There is no community of mind involved. What is dug up by the Resurrection Men is neither kin nor kind but monstrous, alien—or if kin, it bears only a distant resemblance to them, like the murdered grandfather whom the revolutionaries' children never knew. The revived classic is the Other of the moderns, and the end they propose in studying it is neither to discover their roots nor to sever them. The purpose, rather, is to learn something now quite unknown, to affront present orthodoxies, expose present deficiencies, and read in the once-forgotten past future possibilities.

In history (that is, in modernity), the classic that had before been characterized by its survival now comes to subsist by revival. Characteristic of the historical classic is that it is resurrected and reborn, and therefore also, necessarily, that it has died and been forgotten. A kind of historiography that is the contrary of cultural memory crosses Lethe to recall the classic to life. "It is still not common knowledge," René Wellek notes, "that Goethe, after the international success of *Werther*, fell into comparative oblivion" ("Concept of 'Classicism,'" 112). This fall is not unique. "Is Shakespeare a classic?" Sainte-Beuve asks. "Yes, today he is one for England and for the world, but in the period of Pope he was not" ("What Is a Classic?," 5–6). If Goethe and Shakespeare are typical, if classics are not so much born as born again, the lapse into oblivion becomes a fortunate fall, a condition of classicality. The empty interval enables repetition—that is, revival and return with a difference—and alteration is not something that happens to the classic but belongs to what it is. Perpetually differing from itself, every genuine classic is a neo-classic.

When the interlude of obsolescence is conceived as a discontinuity intrinsic to the idea of a classic, as dark ages that are the necessary condition of a renaissance, it becomes necessary to rethink the idea of universality, for the empty gap constitutive of the neoclassic is precisely the interruption that precludes it from being universal in the sense of permanently enduring. Johnson found it necessary to "revise" Shakespeare because "it is vain to carry wishes beyond the condition of human things; that which must happen to all, has happened to Shakespeare" (*Johnson on Shakespeare*, 112). If death is not accidental but essential to human things, the mortality of Shakespeare's plays, which manifests their particularity and explains the need to edit them, shows that in discontinuous human history universality is but a name. The advent of romanticism and of history brought with it a nominalist delight in concrete particulars and a corollary suspicion of universality that lingers still.[10] For the moderns, there are no universal classics, only local and relative ones. And yet, even if the classic is not universal in the sense of belonging to all times, neither is it strictly local, for whatever time might be its point of origin, the neoclassic always belongs to another and different time as well. If we take the blank interval as belonging essentially to the repetition, then the classic is emphatically not universal or perennial. It is, as it were, deciduous. The classic departs but also returns, periodically though perhaps not regularly, occasionally but not always or in every age.

Borges suggest something like this in his other parable of the classic, less well known than "Pierre Menard": "The Garden of Forking Paths." In this story the question is how to conceive of a book that is "strictly infinite," as Ts'ui Pen's chaotic and incomplete novel *The Garden of Forking Paths* purports to be. Stephen Albert, the sinologist in the story, proposes and rejects several possible conceptions of infinity, among them the continuity we have considered:

10. See Bate, *From Classic to Romantic*, 8.

I imagined as well a Platonic, hereditary work, transmitted
from father to son, in which each new individual adds a chapter
or corrects with pious care the pages of his elders. These conjectures diverted me; but none seemed to correspond, not even
remotely to the contradictory chapters of Ts'ui Pen. In the midst
of this perplexity, I received from Oxford the manuscript you
have examined. I lingered, naturally, on the sentence: "I leave to
the various futures (not to all) my garden of forking paths."
Almost instantly, I understood. [97]

Among the various conceptions of the past, and the conceptions of the classic corresponding to them, two have been considered
here: traditionary continuity and historical discontinuity. It remains
to be considered how and whether they can be reconciled. How
might it be possible, in Gadamer's terms, to dissolve "the abstract
antithesis between tradition and historical research, between history
and the knowledge of it" (*Truth and Method*, 282). How, in other
words, could one think of history as productive of knowledge and
truth rather than the source of the relativism that precludes them?
The remainder of this chapter addresses this question.

We have seen that the past conceived as continuous and indivisible
from the present has as its analogue a classic that is always one and
the same, as Kermode claims. This is a traditionary, enduring, universal classic. "No modern language could aspire to the universality
of Latin," Eliot contends. "No modern language can hope to produce a classic, in the sense I have called Virgil a classic. . . . It is
sufficient that this standard should have been established once for
all" (*On Poetry and Poets*, 73). In contrast to this "once for all," the
past considered historically, as having passed, implies an irreducible
plurality of times, and this conception has as its corollary a decid-

uous classic, which, as Smith claims, is always as different from itself as the different times and cultures in which it returns. "I see no evidence whatsoever to suggest that there is any such entity as 'civilization,'" Scholes too asserts, "or that our cultural history embodies or expresses any single, durable vision" ("Aiming a Canon," 114). Cultural difference precludes classical universality.

Even Eliot admits that the universality of the Virgilian classic has its limits. For him, as for Dante, there comes a point beyond which Virgil cannot go; the classic ends where revelation begins. No major literary critic has maintained more vigorously than Eliot the absoluteness of the distinction between literature and scripture. He mocks "the men of letters who have gone into ecstasies over 'the Bible as literature,' the Bible as 'the noblest monument of English prose.' Those who talk of the Bible as a 'monument of English prose' are merely admiring it as a monument over the grave of Christianity" (*Selected Essays*, 344). Now, in our time, it seems that the wheel has come full circle, for in respect to the relation between literature and scripture, Scholes appears to agree fully with Eliot, though for precisely the opposite reasons. Scholes opposes what he sees as Bennett's "attempt to impose a canon on all humanistic study" ("Aiming a Canon," 102) for two reasons: first, because it is "fundamentally undemocratic" (Bennett's list excludes all non-classic texts); second, because it gives the "monuments of the past . . . a quasi-religious or 'canonical' status" (the list includes the Bible and seems prescriptive) (112). What disturbs Scholes, like Christine Froula and many others, is a pedagogy that conceives "'Great Books' on the model of sacred texts" ("When Eve Reads Milton," 171). The offense lies not just in teaching the Bible as literature but—even more scandalously—literature as the Bible. The time seems right to ask once again, what is the difference? What does it mean to think of a text, any text, as scripture?

"If the 'classics' are to become a canon," Scholes asks, "what will become of the Canon?" ("Aiming a Canon," 115). It is a question reminiscent of Eliot: doesn't teaching a classic as the Bible simply deny the difference of the Bible? This would surely be a legitimate question to put to Bennett—but, also, to Scholes as well. The problem for the catholic and democratic Scholes, unlike the Catholic and royalist Eliot, is that Scholes cannot distinguish the classics from the Bible and still maintain the principle of textual democracy. He does not object to teaching the Bible, of course, and he occasionally exhibits a certain reactionary fondness for the literary classics; but he wants to regard them like "any other text that can be shown to be important from our present historical situation. . . . I want the right as a teacher to study and teach every text critically" (115). Thus, precisely unlike Eliot, Scholes wants to teach scripture and non-scripture the same way, not reverently but critically. Precisely like Bennett, Scholes groups the Bible and the classics together indiscriminately, except that for him every text is to be treated like the meanest graffito.

From both the religious and humanist points of view, this leveling seems the basest heresy, a blasphemous reduction. But for some Christians at least, it is not necessarily so. The move from Eliot's differentiation to Scholes's nondifferentiation rehearses the movement in biblical hermeneutics from Chladenius in the eighteenth century to Schleiermacher and then our own day. Like Ernesti and others before him, Chladenius produced not a universal hermeneutics but one limited to "rational discourses and writings," specifically excluding the Bible. "Much effort has been made over the course of many years to collect rules suitable for the interpretation of Holy Scripture," Chladenius wrote in 1742. "But hermeneutics would do well to acknowledge that it alone does not determine the matter. The Holy Scriptures are a work of God, and many rules that might be applicable to human works cannot be applied here at all. Revelation has its own special criticism" ("Concept of Interpretation," 62).[11]

This distinction among the several kinds of hermeneutics still

---

11. I have emended the translation slightly to make it more grammatical.

obtained when Schleiermacher, renowned as both a classical phi-
lologist and a professor of theology, considered it a half-century
later: "At present there is no general hermeneutics as the art of understanding but only a variety of specialized hermeneutics ("General
Hermeneutics," 73). Though he regarded it as his task to remedy this
lack and provide a general hermeneutics describing the transcendental conditions for understanding any discourse whatever, Schleiermacher was nevertheless wary of the question "whether on account
of the Holy Spirit the Scriptures must be treated in a special way.
This question cannot be answered by a dogmatic decision about
inspiration, because such a decision itself depends upon interpretation" (80). Schleiermacher's response does not foreclose the possibility of a special biblical hermeneutics, but it does indicate that
any special hermeneutics would depend on the general hermeneutics
that he was himself developing. In any case, he certainly did not
regard the generality of his project, comprehending both the classics
and scripture, as in any way betokening religious skepticism.

Gadamer's hermeneutics differs from that of Schleiermacher in a
number of significant respects, but not with regard to its impetus
toward generality. Indeed, Gadamer extends philosophical hermeneutics beyond philology and theology to the understanding of
anything whatever. At this level—the level of universal hermeneutics—it may seem that the question of a specifically biblical mode of
interpretation would simply dissolve. In fact, however, the case is
quite the opposite. "Theologians must never forget that Scripture is
the divine proclamation of salvation," Gadamer warns. "Understanding it, therefore, cannot simply be a scientific or scholarly
exploration of its meaning. Bultmann once wrote, 'The interpretation of the biblical writings is subject to exactly the same conditions
as any other literature.' But the meaning of this statement is ambig-
uous, for the question is whether all literature is not subject to
conditions of understanding other than those formal general ones
that have to be fulfilled in regard to every text" (*Truth and Method*,
331). If Bultmann and Schleiermacher before him are right—that

the conditions of understanding are the same for scripture as they are for literature—then Gadamer's reversal follows necessarily: the conditions of understanding that obtain for scripture obtain for every text. If it is agreed on all sides that the classics are treated like "sacred texts"—in the phrase of both Froula and Scholes—then, whether the secular scriptures are to be demystified or reverenced, it is important to consider what this common phrase implies. What does it mean to conceive of the classic as situated at the intersection of text and scripture?

Scholes's usage of the word "Text" offers a convenient place to start: "In the anthropological sense, 'culture' means the textual web that young people enter as they are born and raised in any particular time and place" ("Aiming a Canon," 112). Again, "What I advocate . . . can be summarized as the critical study of texts in their full historical context" (116). Text means, first, the world, the network of signification, or the cultural web in which children cannot avoid being caught as they are socialized. Second, Text means writing or any other cultural formation that belongs to that web insofar as it is studied anthropologically, critically, and historically. Text, then, refers to both a force impinging on consciousness and an object of self-conscious study. As force, a classic Text is a convention that alters nature, patterning the synapses and emerging thoughtlessly as an autonomic response less like a citation than a cliché. The force of the classic Text, to borrow Samuel Johnson's words, "is so great, as to take possession of the memory by a kind of violence, and produce effects almost without the intervention of the will" (*Rambler*, 22). Investigated anthropologically or sociologically, the classic Text becomes an object, since its force is investigated from a distance that serves to immunize the investigators and thereby guarantee the truth and objectivity of their conclusions. At a historical distance, the classic Text is an object of nostalgia (something valuable that was lost), or an object of contempt (something worthless that has been superseded), or merely an object of curiosity that research recovers. In every case, the critical self-consciousness of the anthropologist or historian converts a classical Text into an object whose sociocultural force is registered, if at all, only on others.

Corresponding to the Text as object and force is Scripture as dogma and claim. Scripture is the contrary of Text insofar as Scripture as such is true and applicable to its readers. Studied anthropologically, the classic Text is quasi-aesthetic, something like fiction or poetry: it is neither true nor false because (unlike the anthropologist's own writing) it makes no truth-claim. Likewise, read historically from a historical distance, a classic Text may indicate, betray, or express volumes; but it cannot say anything at all to the historian because of the discontinuity that separates them. Scripture, however, addresses its reader, and does so as both dogma and claim.

Regarded as dogma, Scripture embodies or authorizes a set of explicit, permanent principles that are eternally self-identical, universally true, and therefore applicable to the thought and conduct of every reader without exception. As unobjectified force, the classic Text exerts an unconscious influence; seen as dogma, the classical Scripture embodies a rule to be consciously observed, a standard defining orthodoxy and heresy, imitation and originality. It consists of eternal truths or a pack of lies, but at any rate of a group of determinate, univocal doctrines. Dogma is classical Scripture condensed into propositions, objectified, and raised to consciousness— that is, rendered susceptible of rational belief and doubt. Conceived as a claim, by contrast, classical Scripture is not merely unobjectified (like textual force) but unobjectifiable. Scripture means its reader. That it does so is constitutive of what it is. As dogma, Scripture means something abstract, addressed to all readers in general (or to the general reader). As claim, however, the classic Scripture pertains to each reader, in the concrete and in the second person.[12] It is what

12. I concur with Gerald Bruns that the distinction between canonical and non-canonical, scripture and non-scripture, "is a distinction between texts that are forceful in a given situation and those which are not. From a hermeneutical standpoint, in which the relation of a text to a situation is always of primary interest, the theme of canonization is *power*" ("Canon and Power," 67).

Rilke hears in the "Archaic Torso of Apollo": "Du mußt dein Leben ändern"—a pointed mandate implying an obligation that is unspecified because it is to be fulfilled in a different way by each person to whom it is addressed. There is no distance here; the address is immediate and personal. As Scriptural claim, the classic means you—*de te fabula narratur*—and thus its meaning is essentially unrestricted and limitlessly plural. Since its readers are part of what it means, the classic as Scriptural claim is not subject to historical research: the historical context of the classic is essentially open, and its time is always continuous with the reader's own. For the same reason, what classic Scripture claims cannot be dogmatically fixed in abstract propositions to be affirmed or denied.

To situate the classic at the juncture of Text and Scripture is to suggest that it be conceived as at once force and object, dogma and claim. These four "moments" provide the rudiments of a dialectical framework for thinking about the classic. Isolated, any one of them is merely partial and incomplete. But what understanding of the classic would be conceptually whole? Is it possible today to formulate a unitary conception of the classic that would be comprehensive and noncontradictory? The four moments comprising the classic cannot simply be added up or ecumenically unified in a coherent notion of the classic, for Text and Scripture in addition to being opposed to each other are self-divided as well. The very idea of a textual web as a force in which all are caught calls into question the objectivity of those who treat it as an object of knowledge that affects only others; conversely, precisely insofar as the textual anthropologists can be objective and unaffected by the Text, their objectivity calls the very idea of textual force into question. With respect to Scripture, likewise, the power of its claim on every reader in particular precludes regarding it as an implicit system of general, cognitively justifiable scriptural doctrines; conversely, from the viewpoint of dogma, a scriptural claim that is constitutively incapable of being embodied in determinate, valid propositions cannot properly be called knowledge at all.

Text and Scripture are self-divided, then, and cannot be summarily unified; but this very self-division also enables the four moments to pair themselves horizontally as well as vertically. Text-as-object and Scripture-as-dogma are both intentional correlates of a critical awareness, that of the anthropologist or theologian. Correlatively, Text-as-force is analogous to Scripture-as-claim in that both are extra-critical, either above criticism or below it. Force and claim are passions that the subject endures rather than objects of its intentional acts. Within the critical realm, the interpreter interrogates the classic as object and dogma; conversely, within the extra-critical realm, the classic-as-force-and-claim marks the limits of the interpreter's own capacity for critical reflection. Text and Scripture are divided against themselves in complementary ways. Both consist of a critical and an extra-critical moment, and this complementarity raises the final question of the classic.

What is the relation between truth and power, between what is and what is not subject to critique? In our time, the skeptical answer is most familiar: power and truth are antithetical, and power is the more powerful. The function of critique is to expose truth as the deluded expression of power, of the extra-critical. This answer can be understood in Nietzschean fashion (as asserting that truth can in every case be reduced to power) or in Cartesian fashion (as asserting that critique's claim to truth is invulnerable to such reduction). In any case, the skeptical answer is paradoxical insofar as the exposure of truth itself claims to be exempt from exposure. Because of its self-contradiction, this paradox blocks the attempt to formulate a coherent conception of the classic. For precisely that reason, however, to affirm the coherence of the classic would require our becoming skeptical of the very antithesis upon which the skeptical paradox depends: in Gadamer's terms, the antithesis between history and the knowledge of it, and in our terms, that between force and claim on the one hand and dogma and object on the other. If the classic is at once Text and Scripture, it is not the case that critical reflection always precludes reverence and obedience, that voluntary and involuntary submission always prevents genuine critique, or that the discontinuity from the classic that is the condition of criticizing it severs our continuity and sameness with the classic that is its power. To speak of scriptural Text or textual Scripture—to speak of the classic—is to deny that truth and power are merely antithetical. Every orthodoxy must repress the questions that threaten it, and the new orthodoxy of suspicion must silence the classic. For if truth is in every case the deluded expression of power, the question of the classic is whether power, for just that reason, is the unwitting accomplice of truth.

WORKS CITED

Aldrich, Virgil C. "Mirrors, Pictures, Words, Perceptions." *Philosophy* 55 (1980): 39–56.

Apel, Karl-Otto. *Towards a Transformation of Philosophy*, trans. Glyn Adey and David Frisby. London: Routledge and Kegan Paul, 1980.

Arendt, Hannah. *Lectures on Kant's Political Philosophy*, ed. Ronald Beiner. Chicago: University of Chicago Press, 1982.

Bagwell, Timothy. *American Formalism and the Problem of Interpretation*. Houston: Rice University Press, 1986.

Barthes, Roland. *S/Z*, trans. Richard Miller. New York: Hill and Wang, 1974.

Bate, Walter Jackson. *From Classic to Romantic: Premises of Taste in Eighteenth-Century England*. New York: Harper and Row, 1946.

Bennett, William. "The Shattered Humanities." *Wall Street Journal*, 31 Dec. 1982, 17.

Benveniste, Emile. *Problems in General Linguistics*, trans. Mary E. Meek. Coral Gables: University of Miami Press, 1971.

Bernstein, Richard. "From Hermeneutics to Praxis." In *Hermeneutics and Modern Philosophy*, ed. Brice Wachterhauser, 87–110. Albany: State University of New York Press, 1986.

Betti, Emilio. "Hermeneutics as the General Methodology of the *Geisteswissenschaften*," trans. and ed. Josef Bleicher. In *Contemporary Hermeneutics: Hermeneutics as Method, Philosophy, and Critique*, by Josef Bleicher, 51–94. London: Routledge and Kegan Paul, 1980.

Black, Max. "Metaphor." Reprinted in *Philosophy Looks at the Arts: Contemporary Readings in Aesthetics*, ed. Joseph Margolis, 216–35. New York: Scribner's, 1962.

Bleicher, Josef. *Contemporary Hermeneutics: Hermeneutics as Method, Philosophy, and Critique*. London: Routledge and Kegan Paul, 1980.

Bloom, Allan. *The Closing of the American Mind*. New York: Simon and Schuster, 1987.

Bloom, Harold. *The Anxiety of Influence: A Theory of Poetry*. London: Oxford University Press, 1973.

Booth, Wayne. *Critical Understanding: The Powers and Limits of Pluralism*. Chicago: University of Chicago Press, 1979.

Borges, Jorge Luis. "The Garden of Forking Paths." In *Ficciones*, ed. Anthony Kerrigan, 89–101. New York: Grove, 1962.

Boswell, James. *Life of Johnson*, Rev. ed. London: Oxford University Press, 1953.

Bruns, Gerald. "Canon and Power in the Hebrew Scriptures." In *Canons*, ed. Robert von Hallberg, 65–83. Chicago: University of Chicago Press, 1983.

———. *Inventions: Writing, Textuality, and Understanding in Literary History*. New Haven: Yale University Press, 1982.

Burke, Edmund. *Reflections on the Revolution in France*, ed. Conor Cruise O'Brien. Harmondsworth: Penguin, 1968.

Caputo, John. *Radical Hermeneutics: Repetition, Deconstruction, and the Hermeneutic Project*. Bloomington: Indiana University Press, 1987.

Cassirer, Ernst. *Language*. Vol. 1 of *The Philosophy of Symbolic Forms*, trans. Ralph Manheim. New Haven: Yale University Press, 1955.

———. "Structuralism in Modern Linguistics." *Word* 1 (1945): 99–120.

Chesterfield, Lord. *The Letters of Philip Dormer Stanhope 4th Earl of Chesterfield*, ed. Bonamy Dobrée. London: Eyre and Spottiswoode, 1932.

Chladenius, Johann Martin. "On the Concept of Interpretation." In *The Hermeneutics Reader*, ed. Kurt Mueller-Vollmer, 55–63. New York: Continuum, 1985.

Chomsky, Noam. *Aspects of a Theory of Syntax*. Cambridge: MIT Press, 1969.

———. *Cartesian Linguistics: A Chapter in the History of Rationalist Thought*. New York: Harper and Row, 1966.

———. *Language and Mind*. Enlarged ed. New York: Harcourt Brace Jovanovich, 1972.

Clarke, D. S. *Principles of Semiotic*. London: Routledge and Kegan Paul, 1987.

Cohan, Steven M., et al. "Not a Good Idea: The New Curriculum at Syracuse." Mimeo draft.

Culler, Jonathan. *Ferdinand de Saussure*. Rev. ed. Ithaca: Cornell University Press, 1980.

———. *The Pursuit of Signs: Semiotics, Literature, Deconstruction*. Ithaca: Cornell University Press, 1981.

———. *Structuralist Poetics: Structuralism, Linguistics, and the Study of Literature.* Ithaca: Cornell University Press, 1975.

Dallmayr, Fred R. *Language and Politics: Why Does Language Matter to Political Philosophy?* Notre Dame: University of Notre Dame Press, 1984.

Deely, John. *Introducing Semiotic: Its History and Doctrine.* Bloomington: Indiana University Press, 1982.

De Man, Paul. *Allegories of Reading: Figural Language in Rousseau, Nietzsche, Rilke, and Proust.* New Haven: Yale University Press, 1979.

Derrida, Jacques. *Of Grammatology,* trans. Gayatri Spivak. Baltimore: Johns Hopkins University Press, 1976.

———. "The Parergon," trans. Craig Owens. *October* 9 (1979): 3–41.

———. *Spurs: Nietzsche's Styles,* trans. Barbara Harlow. Chicago: University of Chicago Press, 1978.

———. "White Mythology: Metaphor in the Text of Philosophy." *New Literary History* 6 (1974): 5–74.

Dilthey, Wilhelm. *Selected Writings,* ed. and trans. H. P. Rickman. Cambridge: Cambridge University Press, 1976.

Eco, Umberto. *A Theory of Semiotics.* Bloomington: Indiana University Press, 1976.

Eliot, T. S. *On Poetry and Poets.* London: Farrar, Straus and Giroux, 1943.

———. *Selected Essays.* New York: Harcourt, Brace and World, 1960.

Fleischmann, Wolfgang Bernard. "Classicism." In *The Princeton Encyclopedia of Poetry and Poetics,* ed. Alexander Preminger, Frank J. Warnke, and O. B. Hardison, Jr., 136–41. Princeton: Princeton University Press, 1974.

Foucault, Michel. *The Order of Things: An Archaeology of the Human Sciences.* New York: Vintage, 1973.

Freud, Sigmund. *The Interpretation of Dreams,* trans. and ed. James Strachey. New York: Avon, 1965.

Frings, Manfred S., ed. *Heidegger and the Quest for Truth.* Chicago: Quadrangle, 1968.

Froula, Christine. "When Eve Reads Milton: Undoing the Canonical Economy." In *Canons,* ed. Robert von Hallberg, 149–75. Chicago: University of Chicago Press, 1983.

Gadamer, Hans-Georg. "Anschauung und Anschaulichkeit." *Neue Hefte für Philosophie* 18/19 (1980): 1–14.

————. *Hegel's Dialectic: Five Hermeneutical Studies*, trans. P.
  Christopher Smith. New Haven: Yale University Press, 1967.
————. *Kleine Schriften*. Vol. 2, *Interpretationen*. 2d ed. Tübingen:
  J. C. B. Mohr (Paul Siebeck), 1979.
————. *Kleine Schriften*. Vol. 4, *Variationen*. Tübingen: J. C. B. Mohr
  (Paul Siebeck), 1977.
————. "On the Problematic Character of Aesthetic Consciousness,"
  trans. E. Kelley. *Graduate Faculty Philosophy Journal* 9 (1982): 31–40.
————. *Philosophical Hermeneutics*, trans. and ed. David E. Linge.
  Berkeley and Los Angeles: University of California Press, 1976.
————. *Reason in the Age of Science*, trans. Frederick G. Lawrence.
  Cambridge: MIT Press, 1981.
————. *Truth and Method*, revised translation by Joel Weinsheimer and
  Donald G. Marshall. New York: Seabury Press, 1989.
Goodman, Nelson. *Languages of Art: An Approach to a Theory of
  Symbols*. Indianapolis: Bobbs-Merrill, 1968.
Gras, Vernon W., ed., *European Literary Theory and Practice: From
  Existential Phenomenology to Structuralism*. New York: Delta, 1973.
Gumbrecht, Hans Ulrich. "'Phoenix from the Ashes' or: From Canon to
  Classic." *New Literary History* 20 (1988): 141–63.
Habermas, Jürgen. "The Hermeneutic Claim to Universality," trans. and
  ed. Josef Bleicher. In *Contemporary Hermeneutics: Hermeneutics as
  Method, Philosophy, and Critique*, by Joseph Bleicher, 181–211.
  London: Routledge and Kegan Paul, 1980.
Hartman, Geoffrey. *The Fate of Reading and Other Essays*. Chicago:
  University of Chicago Press, 1975.
Hegel, G. W. F. *Aesthetics: Lectures of Fine Art*, trans. T. M. Knox.
  Oxford: Clarendon Press, 1975.
Heidegger, Martin. *Basic Writings*, ed. and trans. David Farrell Krell.
  New York: Harper and Row, 1977.
————. *Being and Time*, trans. John Macquarrie and Edward Robinson.
  New York: Harper and Row, 1962.
————. *Introduction to Metaphysics*, trans. Ralph Manheim. New
  Haven: Yale University Press, 1959.
————. *Kant and the Problem of Metaphysics*, trans. James S. Churchill.
  Bloomington: Indiana University Press, 1962.
————. *Poetry, Language, Thought*, trans. Albert Hofstadter. New York:
  Harper and Row, 1971.
Hinman, Lawrence. "Quid Facti or Quid Juris: The Fundamental

Ambiguity of Gadamer's Understanding of Hermeneutics." *Philosophy and Phenomenological Research* 40 (1980): 512–35.

Hirsch, E. D., Jr. "Against Theory?" In *Against Theory: Literary Studies and the New Pragmatism*, ed. W. J. T. Mitchell, 48–52. Chicago: University of Chicago Press, 1982.

———. *The Aims of Interpretation*. Chicago: University of Chicago Press, 1976.

———. "'Cultural Literacy' Does Not Mean 'Canon.'" *Salmagundi* 72 (1986): 117–24.

———. *Cultural Literacy: What Every American Needs to Know*. New York: Vintage, 1988.

———. *Validity in Interpretation*. New Haven: Yale University Press, 1967.

Hjelmslev, Louis. *Prolegomena to a Theory of Language*, trans. Francis J. Whitfield. Madison: University of Wisconsin Press, 1969.

Hoy, David. *The Critical Circle: Literature, History, and Philosophical Hermeneutics*. Berkeley and Los Angeles: University of California Press, 1978.

Hulme. T. E. "Classicism and Romanticism." In *Speculations: Essays of Humanism and the Philosophy of Art*, ed. Herbert Read, 113–40. London: Routledge and Kegan Paul, 1949.

Humboldt, Wilhelm von. *On Language: The Diversity of Human Language-Structure and Its Influence on the Mental Development of Mankind*, trans. Peter Heath. Cambridge: Cambridge University Press, 1988.

Jameson, Fredric. *The Political Unconscious*. Ithaca: Cornell University Press, 1984.

———. *The Prison-House of Language: A Critical Account of Structuralism and Russian Formalism*. Princeton: Princeton University Press, 1972.

Johnson, J. W. "The Classics and John Bull." In *England in the Restoration and Early Eighteenth Century: Essays on Culture and Society*. ed. H. T. Swedenberg, Jr. Berkeley and Los Angeles: University of California Press, 1972.

———. *The Formation of English Neo-Classical Thought*. Princeton: Princeton University Press, 1967.

Johnson, Samuel. *Johnson on Shakespeare. The Yale Edition of the Works of Samuel Johnson*, vol. 7, ed. Arthur Sherbo. New Haven: Yale University Press, 1968.

————. *The Rambler. The Yale Edition of the Works of Samuel Johnson*, vol. 3, ed. W. J. Bate and Albrecht B. Strauss. New Haven: Yale University Press, 1969.

Juhl, Peter D. *Interpretation: An Essay in the Philosophy of Literary Criticism*. Princeton: Princeton University Press, 1980.

Kant, Immanuel. *Critique of Judgment*, trans. J. H. Bernard. New York: Hafner, 1951.

————. *Critique of Pure Reason*, trans. Norman Kemp Smith. London: Macmillan, 1961.

————. *Kant's Political Writings*, ed. Hans Reiss and trans. H. B. Nisbet. Cambridge: Cambridge University Press, 1971.

Kermode, Frank. *The Classic: Literary Images of Permanence and Change*. New York: Viking, 1975.

Knapp, Steven, and Walter Benn Michaels. "Against Theory." *Critical Inquiry* 8 (1982): 723–42.

Kristeva, Julia. *Desire in Language: A Semiotic Approach to Literature and Art*, ed. Leon S. Roudiez and trans. Leon S. Roudiez, Thomas Gora, and Alice Jardine. New York: Columbia University Press, 1980.

Kuhn, Thomas. *The Structure of Scientific Revolutions*. 2d ed. Chicago: University of Chicago Press, 1970.

Lipking, Lawrence. "Aristotle's Sister: A Poetics of Abandonment." In *Canons*, ed. Robert von Hallberg, 85–105. Chicago: University of Chicago Press, 1983.

Locke, John. *An Essay Concerning Human Understanding*, ed. Alexander Campbell Fraser. 2 vols. New York: Dover, 1955.

Lyotard, Jean-François, and Jean-Loup Thébaud. *Just Gaming*, trans. Wlad Godzich. Theory and History of Literature, vol. 20. Minneapolis: University of Minnesota Press, 1985.

Margolis, Joseph. "The Human Voice of Semiotics." Forthcoming.

————. ed. *Philosophy Looks at the Arts: Contemporary Readings in Aesthetics*, 1st ed. New York: Scribner's, 1962.

Merleau-Ponty, Maurice. *Signs*, trans. Richard C. McCleary. Evanston: Northwestern University Press, 1964.

Michelfelder, Diane P., and Richard Palmer, eds. *Dialogue and Deconstruction: The Gadamer-Derrida Encounter*. Albany: State University of New York Press, 1989.

Mitchell, W. J. T., ed. *Against Theory: Literary Studies and the New Pragmatism*. Chicago: University of Chicago Press, 1982.

Mueller-Vollmer, Kurt. *The Hermeneutics Reader.* New York: Continuum, 1985.

Murray, Michael. *Modern Critical Theory: A Phenomenological Introduction.* The Hague: Nijhoff, 1975.

Nietzsche, Friedrich. *On the Genealogy of Morals,* trans. Walter Kaufmann and R. J. Hollingdale. New York: Vintage, 1967.

———. *The Use and Abuse of History,* trans. Adrian Collins. New York: Bobbs-Merrill, 1949.

Noakes, Susan. "Hermeneutics and Semiotics: Betti's Debt to Peirce." In *Semiotics 1982* (Proceedings of the Semiotic Society annual meeting). New York: Plenum, 1985.

———. "Literary Semiotics and Hermeneutics: Towards a Taxonomy of the Interpretant." *American Journal of Semiotics* 3, no. 3 (1985): 109–19.

———. *Timely Reading: Between Exegesis and Interpretation.* Ithaca: Cornell University Press, 1988.

O'Brien, Mary. "Feminism and the Politics of Education." *Interchange* 17 (1986): 91–110.

Palmer, Richard. *Hermeneutics: Interpretation Theory in Schleiermacher, Dilthey, Heidegger, and Gadamer.* Evanston: Northwestern University Press, 1969.

Polanyi, Michael. *Personal Knowledge: Towards a Post-Critical Philosophy.* Chicago: University of Chicago Press, 1958.

Pope, Alexander. *The Poems of Alexander Pope,* ed. John Butt. New Haven: Yale University Press, 1963.

Putnam, Hilary. *Philosophical Papers.* Vol. 2, *Mind, Language and Reality.* Cambridge: Cambridge University Press, 1975.

Ricoeur, Paul. *The Conflict of Interpretations: Essays in Hermeneutics,* ed. Don Ihde. Evanston: Northwestern University Press, 1974.

———. *Freud and Philosophy: An Essay on Interpretation,* trans. Denis Savage. New Haven: Yale University Press, 1970.

———. *Hermeneutics and the Human Sciences: Essays on Language, Action and Interpretation,* ed. and trans. John B. Thompson. Cambridge: Cambridge University Press, 1981.

———. *Interpretation Theory: Discourse and the Surplus of Meaning.* Fort Worth: Texas Christian University Press, 1976.

———. "Metaphor and the Main Problem of Hermeneutics." *New Literary History* 6 (1974): 95–110.

———. *The Rule of Metaphor,* trans. Robert Czerny, Kathleen

McLaughlin, and John Costello, S.J. Toronto: University of Toronto Press, 1977.

———. *The Symbolism of Evil*. Boston: Beacon, 1957.

Sainte-Beuve, Charles A. "What Is a Classic?" In *Selected Essays*, trans. and ed. Francis Steegmuller and Norbert Guterman, 1–12. Garden City, N.Y.: Doubleday, 1963.

Saussure, Ferdinand de. *Course in General Linguistics*, ed. Charles Bally and Albert Sechehaye and trans. Wade Baskin. New York: McGraw-Hill, 1966.

Schleiermacher, Friedrich. "General Hermeneutics." In *The Hermeneutics Reader*, ed. Kurt Mueller-Vollmer, 73–85. New York: Continuum, 1985.

———. "*The Hermeneutics*: Outline of the 1819 Lectures," trans. Jan Wojcik and Roland Haas. *New Literary History* 10 (1978): 1–29.

Scholes, Robert. "Aiming a Canon at the Curriculum." *Salmagundi* 72 (1986): 101–17.

———. *Textual Power: Literary Theory and the Teaching of English*. New Haven: Yale University Press, 1985.

Scholes, Robert, Nancy R. Comley, and Gregory L. Ulmer. *Text Book: An Introduction to Literary Language*. New York: St. Martin's, 1988.

Shelley, Percy Bysshe. "A Defense of Poetry." In *Critical Theory Since Plato*, ed. Hazard Adams, 499–513. New York: Harcourt Brace Jovanovich, 1971.

Sinha, Chris. *Language and Representation: A Socio-Naturalistic Approach to Human Development*. New York: Harvester, 1988.

Smith, Barbara H. "Contingencies of Value." In *Canons*, ed. Robert von Hallberg, 5–39. Chicago: University of Chicago Press, 1983.

Sontag, Susan. *Against Interpretation and Other Essays*. New York: Farrar, Straus and Giroux, 1961.

Strauss, Leo. *Liberalism Ancient and Modern*. New York: Basic Books, 1968.

Tarski, Alfred. "The Semantic Conception of Truth." In *Readings in Philosophical Analysis*, ed. Herbert Feigl and Wilfrid Sellars, 52–84. New York: Appleton-Century-Crofts, 1949.

Todorov, Tzvetan. *Symbolism and Interpretation*, trans. Catherine Porter. Ithaca: Cornell University Press, 1982.

Velkley, Richard L. "Gadamer and Kant: The Critique of Modern Aesthetic Consciousness in *Truth and Method*." *Interpretation* 9 (1981): 353–64.

Voloshinov, V. N. *Marxism and the Philosophy of Language*, trans.
Ladislav Matejka and I. R. Titunik. Cambridge: Harvard University
Press, 1986.

Von Hallberg, Robert, ed. *Canons*. Chicago: University of Chicago Press,
1983.

Wachterhauser, Brice, ed. *Hermeneutics and Modern Philosophy*. Albany:
State University of New York Press, 1986.

Warnke, Georgia. *Gadamer: Hermeneutics, Tradition and Reason*.
Stanford: Stanford University Press, 1987.

Weinsheimer, Joel. *Gadamer's Hermeneutics: A Reading of "Truth and
Method."* New Haven: Yale University Press, 1985.

———. "The Heresy of Metaphrase." *Criticism* 24 (1982): 309–26.

———. "Hermeneutic Semiotics and Peirce's 'Ethics of Terminology.'"
Forthcoming in *Semiotica*.

———. *Imitation*. London: Routledge and Kegan Paul, 1984.

———. "'London' and the Fundamental Problem of Hermeneutics."
Critical Inquiry 9 (1982): 303–22.

———. "Mrs. Siddons, the Tragic Muse, and the Problem of *As*." *Journal
of Aesthetics and Art Criticism* 36 (1978): 317–29.

———. "Writing about Literature, and through It." *Boundary* 2, 10
(1982): 69–91.

Wellek, René. "The Term and Concept of "Classicism' in Literary
History." In *Aspects of the Eighteenth Century*, ed. Earl R. Wasserman,
105–28. Baltimore: Johns Hopkins University Press.

Wimsatt, W. K. *The Verbal Icon: Studies in the Meaning of Poetry*.
Lexington: University Press of Kentucky, 1954.

Winckelmann, Johann Joachim. *History of Ancient Art*, trans. G. Henry
Lodge. 4 vols. in 2. New York: Ungar, 1968.

Wittgenstein, Ludwig. *Philosophical Investigations*, trans. G. E. M.
Anscombe. New York: Macmillan, 1953.

Wordsworth, William. *Prose Works*, ed. W. J. B. Owen and J. B. Smyser.
Oxford: Clarendon Press, 1974.

Wright, Kathleen. "Gadamer: The Speculative Structure of Language." In
Hermeneutics and Modern Philosophy, ed. Brice Wachterhauser, 193–
218. Albany: State University of New York Press, 1986.

Wyschogrod, Michael. *Kierkegaard and Heidegger: The Ontology of
Existence*. New York: Humanities Press, 1954.

Young, Edward. *Conjectures on Original Compositon*. 1759. Reprint.
Leeds: Scolar Press, 1966.

INDEX

A